WANT
DO
GET

Merlin Goldman

A SCREENWRITER'S MANUAL

Miracle Fish

First published 2024 by Miracle Fish.

978-1-9160646-9-0

Merlin Goldman is hereby identified as author of this work in accordance with section 77 of the Copyright, Designs and Patents Act 1988. The author has asserted his moral rights.

You may not copy, store, distribute, transmit, reproduce or otherwise make available this publication (or any part of it) in any form, or binding or by any means (print, electronic, digital, optical, mechanical, photocopying, recording or otherwise), without the prior written permission of the publisher. Any person who does any un-authorised act in relation to this publication may be liable to criminal prosecution and civil claims for damages.

A catalogue record for this book is available from the British Library.

Illustrations by Seb Aird.
Designed by James Pople.
Proofread by Joanna Peios.

Printed and bound in the United Kingdom by Ingram Spark.

CONTENTS

01. INTRODUCTION — 8

Precursor — 11
Methodology — 12
Rules — 14
Bias — 15
What Are Stories For? — 15
Change — 17

02. IDEATION — 20

Genre — 22
Write Who You Know — 23
Write What You Know — 24
Research — 26
Write To Discover — 28
  Pantsing — 28
  Free Writing — 29
  Music — 29
  Three Random Things — 31
  Trouble At Work — 32
  Bad Apples — 33
  Fish Out Of Water — 35
  History — 36
Premise — 38
Anger Is An Energy — 39
Constraints — 39
  Time — 40
  Location — 40
  Characters — 41
  Genre — 41
  Read A Newspaper — 42
Find An Image — 43
Objects — 43
Shaping — 44

Research	**44**
Elements Of Circumstance	**45**
Logline	**46**
Sculpting	**48**
Skeleton Document	48
Objectives	53
Outline	53
Character Descriptions	53
Plot Table	54
Sequences	**56**
Current Situation	57
Trigger Event	57
Character's Objective	57
Character's Options	58
Choice Taken	58
Interaction	59
Result	59
New Situation	59
Waypoints	**63**
Scene Sheet	**64**
Carding	**66**
Oral Telling	**68**
Workflow	**68**
Theme	**69**
Can Nerds Find Love?	71
Associations	**75**
Transformations	**77**
Protagonist vs Antagonist	**79**
Aphorisms	**82**
Idioms	**83**

03. STRUCTURE — 84

Shape	**86**
Acts	**87**
Symmetry	**90**
Circles	**102**
Music	**106**
Storysaurus	**108**
Opening And Closing Images	**110**

04. PLOT   114

Two Plots — 116
Want — 120
    Want Change — 121
    Don't Want Change — 121
    Want Knowledge — 122
    The Prize Method — 123
Do — 125
Get — 126
Worlds — 129

05. THE MIND PLOT   134

The Hero's Journey — 137
Act 1 — 144
    Home World — 144
    Status Quo — 144
    Dark Clouds — 145
    Flaw Exposed — 145
    Save The Cat — 146
    Inciting Incident — 146
    Antagonist — 147
    Bad Behaviour — 147
    Cold Feet — 148
    Leave Home — 148
Act 2 — 149
    Alien World — 149
    Mentor — 150
    Friends And Enemies — 151
    Midpoint — 151
    Moment Of Reflection — 153
    Another Alien World — 154
    Ultimate Test And Significant Death — 154
Act 3 — 155
    Shadow World — 156
    All Or Nothing — 156
    Suit Up — 157
    Final Fight — 157
    It Takes Two — 159
    Outcome — 160
    Reward — 161

Inciting Incident And The Final Fight — 166
    Eager — 167
    Unconfident — 167
    Accidental — 168
    Foolhardy — 168
    Reckless — 169
    Cursed — 169
Significant Death And Pseudo Death — 170

06. THE HEART PLOT — 172

Act 1 — 175
Act 2a — 176
Act 2b — 177
Act 2c — 178
Act 3 — 179

07. EXCEPTIONS — 180

Chaos Stories — 182
Coincidence — 183
Moment Of Wonder — 183
Genre — 185
    Western — 185
Non-Linear Narratives — 187

08. CHARACTER — 192

Monologues — 194
Questions — 195
Memories — 196
The Protagonist — 197
    Interesting — 198
    Selfless — 198
    Relatable — 199
    Want And Need — 200
    Superpower — 201
    Flawed — 202
    Active — 203
    Fallible — 204
    Resilient — 205
    Malleable — 205

Character Arcs — 209
Character Archetypes — 210
- The Hero — 212
- The Mentor — 213
- The Trickster — 215
- The Everyman — 216
- The Herald — 217
- The Gatekeeper — 218
- The Shadow — 219
- The Outsider — 221
- Using Character Archetypes — 222
- Big Characters — 225
- Who's The Hero? — 226
- Webs — 228
- Point Of View — 228
- Revelations — 230
- Flaw — 231
- Positive Flaw — 234

EXTRAS — 236

- Editing — 238
- Detectives — 240
- TV vs Film — 240
- Loss — 241
- Exposition — 242
- Screenwriting Format — 242
- Loglines — 243

APPENDIX — 246

Bibliography — 248
Cloud Of Flaws — 256
Character Archetypes — 258
Acknowledgements — 260

01.

INTRODUCTION

Welcome to *Want Do Get*. This is the book I wished I had when I began writing. I was unemployed, and my mind started coming up with stories. Using a free download of Celtx I started writing stories. One had something to do with sausages, and another resembled *The Red Shoes*. I still have some of those terrible scripts. But they got me going. Celtx announced they were running a competition in partnership with the Montreal Fringe Festival. They put a call out for play scripts from which several were chosen and converted into a play all within twenty-four hours. I knew nothing about story structure or writing plays. But I had a go.

I wrote a play called *Firewall*. Much like *The Matrix* or *Preacher* it anthropomorphised mythical or religious figures, mine did the same – heaven's angels became the firewall that prevented God from being overwhelmed by the thousands of prayers sent upwards. It told the story of a humble burger flipper who leaves his job and family to go on a journey. He faces trials and tribulations and changes of direction and reaches a point of self-realisation along with some conclusion. It was selected and performed as a musical. Unfortunately, I didn't have the funds to travel, but I watched a small clip of the performance.

This small success encouraged me to continue writing. I wrote in coffee shops and pubs after work or at weekends. Firstly, through a Meetup Writing Group which met Monday and Wednesday evenings, along with Sundays. The core members formed a group: initially Knight Writers (when *Knight Rider* was still memorable), then Night Writers, and currently, Write Together – Bristol. The opportunity to sit beside someone who is also trying to form sentences on the page was a great help to me. Through these sessions, I've written (or first drafted) three books, half a dozen plays and a dozen (mostly short) screenplays. The group reads each other's work, watches their plays or readings, and we've organised writing retreats. Most importantly, friendships have formed.

Nothing beats writing to get better at writing. However, there are other things I've done that have helped. The first is reading. As Maureen Lipman, actor and author said at a talk given to my school, 'If you can read, you can write.' When I was a child, my favourite fictional character was Batman. I had the t-shirt (you can see it in my school photographs). I had hundreds of comics: *Batman, Iron Man, The Incredible Hulk, Firestorm, the Nuclear Man* and *X-Men*. After my mother cleared them from her attic, I sold most of them. Reading comics was my informal education in storytelling. A story told in a hundred images – each comic book an episode in a series. I also read books, often detective stories (Agatha Christie or Sir Arthur Conan Doyle) and the choose-your-own-adventure books or whatever our summer reading list from school included.

Following the unexpected 'beginner's luck' confidence boost given by the Celtx competition, I began to read books on writing. This book wouldn't exist without the knowledge I gleaned from them. Or the many courses I attended, in person and online. I've learnt something from each and distilled them here. It's called *Want Do Get* as this neatly summarises the blueprint of most stories. Someone wants something, they do something to try and obtain it, and by the end, you find out if they've got it. It's the classic 3-Act structure, but I'm getting ahead of myself, you'll need to read it to find all this out.

I hope this book provides something different or new to what you've read or understood. I found many of the existing books were in formats that didn't work well for me. They were too dense or too long to get to the point, and their examples were too limited. There were few, if any, diagrams to help illustrate the point. I've written this book in a format that works for me. I hope it works for you too. While the book is focussed on screenwriting, it should apply to other forms such as novels and plays. And you'll find examples from both. And if you take nothing else away, remember: **Want Do Get**.

PRECURSOR

This section is not a prologue, honestly. I know you want to get straight into it. So do I. There's no need to read this book in order. Jump to whichever chapter takes your fancy. This book is called a screenwriter's manual for a reason. When you're stuck, go to the section that may offer a solution. There's no judgement. What works for you, works. A few general notes to bear in mind:

- When I refer to a protagonist, there could be more than one
- When I refer to a hero, they can be any gender
- When I refer to a character, they could be a human, an animal, or an object

METHODOLOGY

The techniques proposed in this section are based on listening, reading, observation, and reverse engineering. Through watching films, TV series, going to plays, reading poetry and books, or later, attending workshops and having discussions with other writers, I recorded much of what is here in a series of blog posts on my website. Sometimes it was something that caught my attention: an odd moment or something like a thing I'd seen before. I generated sufficient material to give talks to my film club. Many of my observations related to how a particular story element was used. These elements of story appear again and again but reinvented or made fresh by being within a different story. And not just by writers. But all those contribute to publishing a story, from dramaturgs to editors to script consultants.

Reverse engineering requires observation while holding a virtual screwdriver. It involves breaking down something complex into its constituent parts (Figure 1). By examining the elements, you can approximate how it was assembled. You then might be able to use the build process to elicit the same outcome as the original. But there's no guarantee. It's unlikely that you want to make the identical object anyway, so your copy's differences should be a positive. But if you recreated a near identical copy, it might not work. Many sequels and remakes fail to live up to their original, either artistically or commercially. However, reverse engineering has revealed many insights into story structure that I'll discuss later.

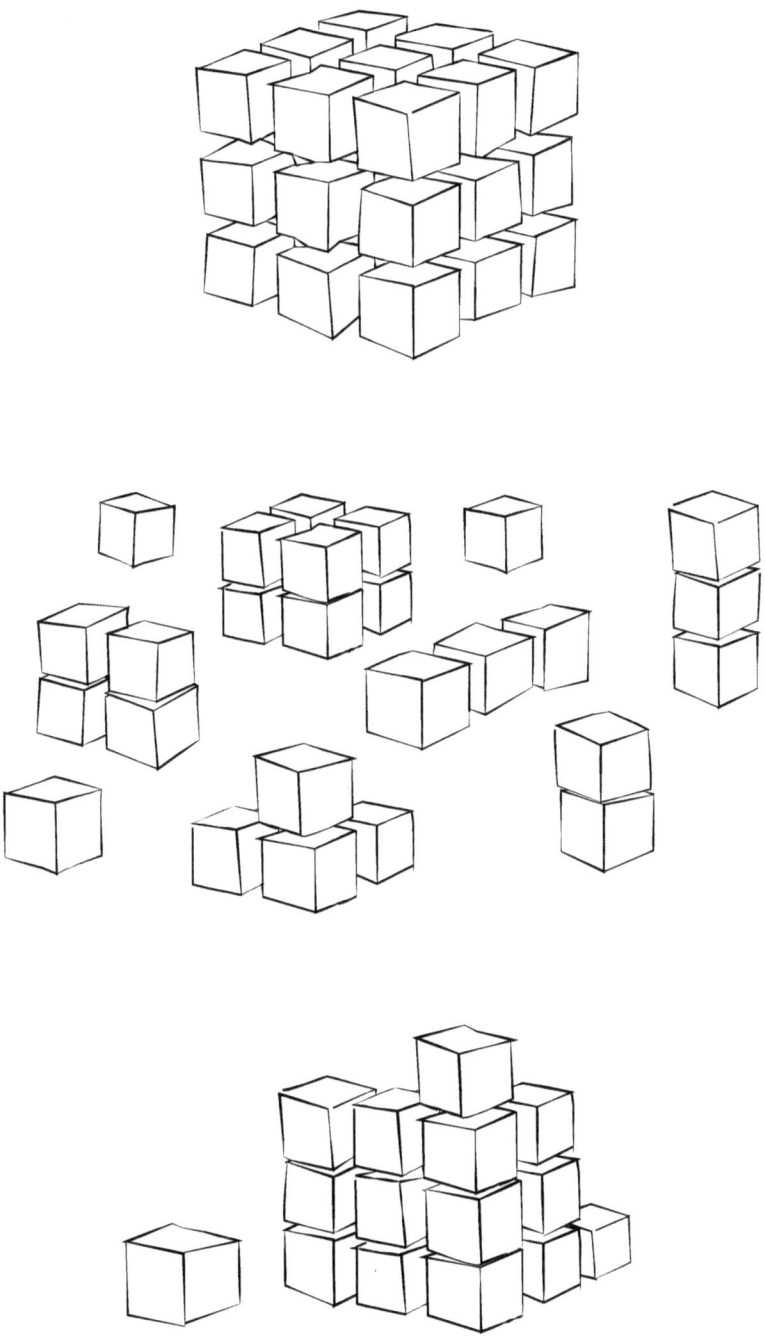

Figure 1: Reverse Engineering.

RULES

There are no rules but I've provided plenty of tools you should find helpful. There's no single route through the forest, but there are a few well-worn paths that others have followed to safety. You can try any of them, and even double back and try a different one. And as this is a fantastical metaphor, you can try several at the same time.

BIAS

We all have inherent biases through our genetics and life experiences. It's our point of view. It informs your voice, that awkward term that describes your unique way of writing. My first plays were heavily influenced by the style of playwrights whose work I'd recently devoured. My first novels contained many autobiographical elements, such as events or individuals. Much of this was done subconsciously. In an interview, Stephen Spielberg was told that he'd replicated his parents' professions (musician and programmer) in *Close Encounters of The Third Kind*. Over time, I began to write less like others and more like myself. I found my voice. To find yours, keep writing.

Writing about ourselves is a natural thing to do. After all, it's the story you know best. But it has risks. Firstly, you will only be able to write about yourself or a version of yourself. Now that needn't be a barrier to success. For example, Ian Rankin stated that his detective, Rebus, is a, 'less good version of himself.' But you may find yourself in a rut that you can't get out of, and the well is starting to run dry. Live a little. Take an evening course, take a holiday, or read non-fiction. New experiences will enrich your story ideas.

WHAT ARE STORIES FOR?

Joseph Campbell was an American academic who studied mythology and proposed the Hero's Journey, a universal story that all stories mimicked, in *The Hero with a Thousand Faces*, published in 1949. It's generated numerous templates for writers and spawned hundreds of books and articles. I'll come back to it in more detail later but in essence, he believed that a single story, the monomyth, was repeated and again in all stories. The only thing that changed was the makeup of the protagonist, but who was always a hero. They always left their homeland, travelled to a dark land, defeated an enemy before returning triumphant. Campbell believed that stories had purpose, several in fact:

1. To create wonder
2. Explain how things work, e.g. seasons
3. Enforce social order
4. A guide for the different stages of life

Leaving number 1 aside, can I argue that 2, 3 and 4 are still relevant? In terms of 2, when telling a young child something, stories do seem to work better than logic. I suppose 3 is particularly obvious in religious texts, and there's a long history of the state using religion to direct public behaviour. But now? When most governments are secular and the number of people who say they are religious keeps falling. And for 4, I think this is an interesting connection, which has some relevance when considering children's literature or biographies. In many ways, wellness and self-help books now fill this function. People, like heroes, have flaws that can prevent them from reaching their goals. But in real life, how often do we address our shortcomings with a mentor and partner with allies to overcome a single bad guy? Rarely.

I think stories have other purposes. To educate seems like a common use of stories. Many fairy tales are morality lessons. They tell us how to behave, perform tasks or spot danger. Before the printing press, information-sharing methods were verbal, with stories sung by wandering minstrels, family elders or preachers. Instructions on how to do something, such as plough a field or plant seeds, surely do not need to be embellished as a story, do they? But if *The Boy Who Cried Wolf* carries the message of not lying about something important, perhaps it's more likely to stick in the memory. You should also consider the nefarious uses of stories, e.g. spreading lies or enrolling in scams. While this has likely always existed (e.g. snake oil salesman), social media has provided a fertile space for fake stories (and facts labelled as fake news).

Above all, what stories do well is engage our attention, often while delivering a message. They work well in advertising but especially in entertainment. While their delivery of a notification may be diminishing, a multi-billion pound industry has formed on telling stories in games, novels, plays, films, and television. And to tell a good story, you need to power it from start to finish. And while the fuel might be a theme, characters, plot etc., they're all to do one thing: facilitate change. And you can live vicariously through those characters, watching them face obstacles, their fears and overcome them, while you sit safely in our seats.

CHANGE

Within every story is an engine driving it forward. Without movement, oil goes bad, and the pistons freeze up. But rather than the motor generating distance, it accumulates change. This forward momentum creates a transformation from one state to another. There are three types of change:

1. The protagonist changes
2. The protagonist changes other people
3. The protagonist changes the world

The mostly common type of change is 1. From zero to hero (*Shazam!*), from soldier to don (*The Godfather*), or farm boy to Jedi (*Star Wars*), we see them resist change. But overcoming challenges, exacerbated by faults in their character, they do change. And they may inspire us to do the same.

In 2 (and 3), the protagonist is an agent of change. They do not change themselves but those around them. These stories can unfold in a light, humorous way, such as *Forrest Gump* or Raymond Babbitt in *Rain Man*. These two characters trigger transformative change in others. Forrest changes history, being present at world-defining events. Raymond makes his brother less selfish.

In 3, the protagonist changes the world. In *The Shawshank Redemption*, Andy Dufresne believes so strongly in his innocence that he changes his world by leaving it. He escapes the prison. Red doesn't believe change is possible for someone like him, but inspired by Andy, he serves his time, and finds him (so a bit of 2).

3 is a common structure for biopics, focussing on the protagonist's whole life or, more likely, the key moments leading up to their global impact. Often the world's set, and they see something wrong with it. Sure of their conviction, their stubbornness pushes them forward. Examples include *Selma*, *Hidden Figures*, and *The Imitation Game*.

But what if a character is not keen to change? What if you're stubborn like Randle McMurphy in *One Flew over the Cuckoo's Nest*? He improves the lives of those around him (2) but refuses to change himself so is lobotomised. In *Pulp Fiction*, Vincent Vega doesn't wish to change his life as a hired gun, so is shot dead. **Change or die.**

NOTES

02.

IDEATION

Ideation is a fancy term for the process of coming up with new ideas (idea plus generation). When writing, where do your ideas come from? Perhaps you have many already. If you don't, how can you generate a few? In this section, I'll discuss different ways to do that. As many writers stick to a particular flavour of story, or genre, we'll start there.

GENRE

Here's a list of some of the most popular:

- Action and Adventure
- Children and Family
- Comedies
- Dramas
- Horror
- Romantic
- Sci-fi and Fantasy
- Sports
- Thrillers
- Western

If you watch a Western, there are certain things you'd expect to see. If you don't see them, you'd probably be disappointed or at the very least, confused. Therefore writers (or directors) are expected to include certain tropes, such as:

- An expansive, barren landscape
- A dress code – riding gear for men, dresses for women
- Horses
- A saloon
- A gunfight

And so on. There's a judgement call in how much of these elements to include without it becoming clichéd.

A popular method to freshen up a stale genre is to mix two together (hybridisation). If mixed throughout we can generate fresh, new worlds e.g. *Cowboy Bebop*, *Serenity* (Western and Sci-fi). Or switch genres at each Act break e.g. *Sorry to Bother You* (Social Drama to Thriller to Horror). Here are two more examples of each type:

Westworld

Westworld, the film from 1973, and much of the TV series first screened in 2016, is set in a futuristic Western-themed amusement park. It blends sci-fi tropes (robots going rogue, corporate excess) and Western imagery to create something different, that is also familiar. There are saloons with pianos, wooden buildings, and gunfights. Early Westerns celebrated the American conquest of the territory and its inhabitants. *Westworld* presents a future world where the subservient (robot) masses rise up to overthrow their complacent, decadent masters.

Get Out

Released in 2017, *Get Out* regained its modest budget multiple times over. The film's about Chris Washington, a black man visiting his white girlfriend's parents for the first time. It is set primarily in their house. Act 1 feels like a crime thriller with an opening scene of a man kidnapped (who reappears later seemingly unharmed). Act 2 moves into psychological thriller territory as Chris is trapped and tortured. In Act 3, the film moves into sci-fi territory, echoing B-movie brainswapping films.

WRITE WHO YOU KNOW

Writing **who** you know is a good place to mine for ideas. And the results will be unique. My early writing included life events and characters based on people I've known. There is nothing wrong with this. It's authentic and specific. Biographies are the purest example, although commercial success is concentrated around celebrities and historical figures. The travelogue has gone the same way as travel has became more accessible and affordable, unless the events are extraordinary e.g. *127 Hours*.

If you're not famous, can you still write about yourself? Of course. Our lived experience is unique and worth recording: people you've met, jobs you've had, and places you've visited. Writing about yourself brings a truthfulness that people value. As it becomes easier to fake who or what you are, authenticity has greater value. Feature films often began with the title card, 'based on true events.' But what if you don't want to write about yourself? What about other people? Family, friends, work colleagues? You'll probably want to changes names and other elements to make them less easily identifiable.

John Cleese and Connie Booth based the owners of the hotel in *Fawlty Towers* on their real life hosts of a seaside hotel in Torquay. They stayed at the hotel in 1971 when he was filming *Monty Python's Flying Circus*. They were amazed at the chilly greeting they received from the proprietors. The other Pythons moved out but John stayed. He described the owner as, 'the most wonderfully rude man I have ever met'.

WRITE WHAT YOU KNOW

This method can also be biographical. After all, most of **what** you know is through experience, whether from events you experience in your life, or reading or listening to others talk about them. We learn about the world through observation and by interacting with it. We learn that our actions have consequences which lead us to re-evaluate our original decisions. And ultimately help us understand how the world works. And by the world, this could mean location, any family, a profession, a community, or a hobby. The activity is the key to this type of story – the what rather than the who. What do you know well? The thing you know better than anyone else?

Most of us have at least one hobby. Could that be something you can mine for ideas? Maybe you play Sunday league football. But so do millions of others. But is your team different in some way, e.g. rubbish, undefeated, gay, or disabled? Did it have a memorable season? The 2015 to 16 season of the English Premier League was unique as Leicester Football Club won it for the first time. The previous season, they'd finished fourteenth. *Moneyball* relates the 2002 US baseball season when Oakland A's – a good team but with a small budget – used statistical analysis to acquire new players. As a result, they won twenty consecutive games, setting the American League record.

The Beach

The Beach is based on the novel by Alex Garland and is about a traveller who finds a map that leads him to a hidden island paradise (The Sanctuary). Alex wrote the book while living in the Philippines and The Sanctuary may be inspired by a hippy resort in the Gulf of Thailand. The story has echoes of *Lord of the Flies*, where a seemingly idyllic paradise hides dark secrets. The dynamics of the individuals within The Sanctuary are richly observed and believable.

While new experiences like going backpacking can generate great stories, this doesn't mean its the only way. Listen to public conversations. Be vigilant. Find opportunities to try something new, meet new people. Watch how people behave and write notes. I have a folder called *Writing Ideas* with 84 notes ranging from hyperlinks to Tweets to one that is a list of random words: missing men, lanterns, ghosts, marigolds. Write what you know better than anyone else through experience. We've always got research to fill any gaps.

RESEARCH

Research is part of every writer's toolkit and can even spark a whole new story idea by itself. Research is the bedrock of accuracy when you're not writing about yourself or someone you know well. Through internet searches, reading books, or interviews, research brings accuracy and new detail to your idea. In pitch meetings, it demonstrates professionalism. Research helps to expand an idea with new story material. The internet is a great tool but what are the alternatives? Do you have access to someone who lived an extraordinary life? Or has an unusual hobby? Ask them for an interview.

What if the person you find is so fascinating, you decide to write a biopic. Are they still alive? Could you cause outrage or be sued for writing without their permission? Or their estate's approval? If you continue, be choosy of the period you pick. It's unusual to cover their whole life (unless it's a book). Find a pivotal moment. *Selma* is about Dr Martin Luther King, Jr.'s campaign to secure equal voting rights, that culminates in a march from Selma. In *Judy*, we see Judy Garland as an exhausted, single mother trying to provide a stable home for her children.

Here are two more:

Stan and Ollie

In this biopic, Stan Laurel and Oliver Hardy arrive in the UK to perform a farewell tour. Like *Logan* or *The Wrestler*, this type of story is called **One Final Battle**. The world views them as finished but they are given one more chance to prove they've still got it. For Logan or Randy 'The Ram' Robinson, their physical strength has diminished through ageing and injury. In *Stan and Ollie*, their golden years are behind them. They are no longer making movies.

Their tour of the UK reignites their love of performing and each other, and affirms their affection in the eyes of the public. But their success is hard won due to Ollie's poor health, long-held grievances, hectic schedule, and small audiences. But they prove they still have the magic.

Belfast

Belfast is about Kenneth Branagh's early life in Northern Ireland during the Troubles. It's told mostly from Buddy's (Kenneth's) point of view and the life events he remembers, imagines, or was told. It's not the coming-of-age story we might expect from the premise. Buddy hardly changes, and is mostly pushed and pulled by others. The person that changes the most is his mother. Initially, she's keen to stay but as the situation worsens, and Catholic families leave, she is persuaded to move to London where her husband has work.

By its nature, autobiographical work lacks perspective and neutrality. But this is what makes biographical work appealing. Stories should show thematic tension between two opposing ideological standpoints with the protagonist at the centre. The protagonist, which could be you, must be challenged and may undergo change. If you're writing about yourself, are you prepared to relive past traumatic events? And is your story as interesting as you think it is to others. If not, you might need to play a bit fast and hard with the truth as well as make it fit into some sort of story structure. Research is a great tool, but can feel a little dry. The trick is to think of it as generating a palette of colours to mix with.

WRITE TO DISCOVER

If you have some or even no idea of what you want to write, or want to flesh out an idea, write to discover. Here are a few different techniques to try:

PANTSING

Pantsing probably relates to the idiom, 'flying by the seat of your pants'. That phrase was first used to describe Douglas Corrigan's flight from the USA to Ireland – a risky endeavour in 1938. The term describes performing a task with little to no preparation. Instead, you make things up on the spot. For many, this is terrifying; for others, thrilling. Pantsing is used by writers with a kernel of an idea who allow their imagination to take them to unexpected places. Ian Rankin, author of the Rebus novels begins with a news snippet and little to no planning. As a result, he'll often not know the identity of the killer until the last few chapters.

Pantsing is closely associated with NaNoWriMo (National Novel Writing Month). During November, thousands of writers worldwide try to write a novel in 30 days. I've participated twice, succeeding the first time and the second with an additional two weeks. They were gruelling, thrilling experiences. To help prepare for each session, I tried to stop the previous one at a point where the scene was halfwritten. Many times, I failed to do this and shut the laptop without knowing what was going to happen next. But somehow, the following day, I'd a find way forward.

FREE WRITING

Pantsing could be considered a focused form of free writing. For my two novels, I knew the main character, a location or two, and the genre. But free writing has no starting point or any boundaries. You simply write, usually by hand, anything that comes to mind. Start with the phrase, 'I am writing?' if you're stuck. And repeat. Eventually, something else should emerge, and your pen will take you to places you most likely didn't expect. Whether what you've generated is either legible or valuable, it can be an excellent warm-up technique. Set a timer for five minutes and just write gobbledegook, you'll feel better for it, and may discover a new story idea or character.

MUSIC

Many advocate the use of music to help them get in the mood to write. Others suggest it negatively affects their rhythm. I prefer to write with wordless music in the background. But could the lyrics of a song, or its form, inspire you to come up with a story idea? After all, many songs tell stories e.g. nursery rhymes. Songs without lyrics can create a feeling or a mood that may inspire you. Here's a few songs that inspired me, if not to write a story, at least play with an idea in my head:

Montreal (The Wedding Present)

This song is about a long-distance love affair with a bittersweet ending. It has a location, Montreal, and two protagonists. One is besotted but the other isn't.

Severed (The Decemberists)

A dark city is visited by a new hero, who arrives as quiet as the night. They were born like an animal in the snow. When no one else will do what needs to be done, they will cut the evil from the world, like cancer from a body.

Horseshoe Crab (Slothrust)

They woke bloody, hungry, thirsty, confused, and unable to understand the world. Maybe they came from water? But doesn't everyone? So why did they feel out of place? They were beautiful and unique, like a seahorse. Or like a horseshoe crab. But was their only purpose to be bled by the world they were born into?

Half Moon Street (Pete and the Pirates)

On a night out, you meet an unusual woman with deep-set eyes. She tells you to meet her on Half Moon Street at midnight. Things progress, and you're embroiled in a world of intoxication, car journeys, speaking in tongues, gold coins, and idiots.

So, keep an ear out for a song that resonates with you at an emotional level, write down your interpretation of what it might mean, and see where that takes you.

THREE RANDOM THINGS

You don't need much to spark an idea; three things can do it. While there are more sophisticated ways of using this technique, e.g. story dice, you can emulate it with just a few prompts. My method is based on the guessing game, Animal, Vegetable, or Mineral:

1. Pick a character (human)
2. Something else living, and
3. An object

You could choose boy, dog, and stick. Now create a scene with them. Perhaps the boy throws the stick for the dog to chase. Or he hits the animal with it? Maybe the dog finds a stick that is, in fact a wand, and brings it to the boy. Or start with a more well known trio:

Superman, Lex Luther, and a bomb

Here's a well-known dynamic. Superman's our human (-like) character, Lex is his adversary, and the object is a bomb, providing a focus for their interaction.

A Police Chief, a shark, and a rifle

This combination is from *Jaws*, of course. You have Brody, the Police Chief (who's scared of water), a sea-bound predator and a weapon, the gun. Here's a few more sets:

- Knight, dragon, and treasure, or
- Princes, brides, and arrows, or
- Cat, mouse, and cheese, or
- Coyote, road runner and boulder/anvil/cliff

TROUBLE AT WORK

A variation on the technique above is to use profession, problem, and solution. You pick a career, give the lead character a problem, and have them try to find a solution – preferably one at odds with their job. This scenario immediately creates conflict. And conflict is the lubricant for a story's engine.

If your protagonist does something that clashes with the norms of their profession, it should generate a heap of tension. How will they hide their activity from colleagues? What would happen if they got caught? If they lost their job, what are the ramifications? Could they lose their house? How would it affect their relationships?

A benefit of starting with this triad is that it allows you to generate material fast. We should all be able to generate a list of jobs we have a sense of what they entail. Even if you don't have first-hand knowledge. But if you need a head start:

- Architect
- Chef
- Civil engineer
- Counsellor
- Doctor
- Electrician
- Fitness instructor
- Gardener and landscaper
- Hairdresser and barber
- Journalist
- Lawyer
- Midwife
- Nurse
- Office manager
- Painter and decorator
- Paramedic
- Police
- Property, housing, and estate agent

- Physiotherapist
- Psychologist
- Public Relations
- Senior care worker
- Teacher
- Travel agent
- Veterinarian
- Waiter or waitress

I've focussed on roles that are not primarily desk-based. It helps to retain visual interest if the protagonist gets out and about a bit. You should see already that many of these have formed the basis of TV shows, e.g. *The Office*, *Law and Order*, *The Responder*, *Teachers*, *Hill Street Blues*, *Silk*, *Call the Midwife*, and *Stath Lets Flats*. And for most, the main character is at odds with professional expectations. If they're really awful, we'd call them bad apples.[1]

BAD APPLES

These rebellious individuals are fascinating to watch. We join them when their bad behaviour is ingrained or we watch their descent. In the latter they're faced with a problem and they make a bad choice that puts them at risk of losing their job. Here are a few examples:

- **Dexter:** a forensic scientist who's also a serial killer
- **Breaking Bad:** a Chemistry teacher who makes illegal drugs
- **The Shield:** police officers that use criminal methods
- **Barry:** a hitman who finds a passion for acting

Let's look at two in more detail:

---

[1]. A bad apple was first used to describe how one poor acting person can corrupt others in a group but has more recently been used to suggest that they're a non-influential outlier.

Ideation.

Dirty Harry

In this series of five films, Clint Eastwood plays Homicide Division Inspector, 'Dirty' Harry Callahan, who regularly ignores standard police practice. His unconventional and violent approach to apprehending criminals resonated with a public who felt criminals were getting away with it. His loner persona within a conformist organisation that relies on teamwork was a box office success. His superiors tolerated his actions as he got results. But despite his brutality and bending of the rules he knew where to draw the line. In *Magnum Force*, Callahan faced a group of police officers more extreme than him who executed criminals who escaped conviction. Callahan hunted them down.

Nurse Jackie

This 2009-15 TV series centred on Jackie Peyton, played by Edie Falco, a nurse in a large, city hospital. It was unique at the time as most shows were male-led and focussed on getting more fame, money, power. Jackie's goal was to manage her complicated life. Jackie was a no-nonsense, experienced, and competent nurse, but with a weakness for painkillers as well as having an extramarital affair. These behaviours were at odds with her profession and threatened to dismantle her personal life.

In these examples, most of the protagonist's colleagues or family believe that they are law-abiding and trustworthy. This makes their transgressive behaviour doubly exciting. So if watching a person that should be good, according to their profession, being bad, is entertaining, can the opposite be true.

Can *bad* individuals trying to be good be interesting? What if our protagonist is on the face of it a bad person but does something good:

- **The Sopranos:** a mafia boss who undertakes therapy
- **Terminator 2: Judgment Day:** a killer cyborg protects its usual prey
- **Banshee:** an ex-convict becomes a town sheriff

It looks like it can. What other situations might there be? A good place to find them is sitcoms. Often the lead character isn't suited to their profession, creating humorous rather than purely dramatic situations. For example:

- **The Office:** David Brent is a people pleaser first, manager last
- **Rev:** about an indecisive, doormat-like priest in an inner-city church
- **Motherland:** a disorganised mother in a world of supermums
- **Ted Lasso:** a jovial college-level American football coach becomes coach of an English Premiership team

FISH OUT OF WATER

In the previous section, I gave examples of individuals whose personality or behaviour didn't fit expectations of their profession. A similar scenario is fish out of water, where the protagonist finds themselves in situation they are ill-equipped to face. In fact, most stories have elements of this but we'll come to that later when we discuss **plot**. But consider:

- **The Matrix:** an office worker leaves his humdrum (virtual) world to find himself in a dystopian wasteland run by an AI
- **The Wizard of Oz:** a bored farm girl travels to a technicolour land of magical creatures

The usefulness of taking the protagonist from their comfortable world to a new, stranger one is that it generates conflict. If you only have a new world as a starting point, you could even work backwards to create an unsuitable protagonist. The resulting combination should create opportunities for surprises, obstacles, learning opportunities, and conflict. These are rich veins you can mine for scenes. The protagonist can bring foreign skills with them. For example, in *Terminator 2: Judgment Day* or *Breaking Bad*, their skills become an advantage that sets them apart and becomes an asset later. Let's look at another:

Witness

In this 1985 film, Harrison Ford plays a detective, John Book, that must protect a witness by living with his Amish family. John is an outsider – single, gruff, and lives in Philadelphia. John struggles to blend into the community of law-abiding, peaceful, religious and polite people.

HISTORY

Historical dramas are a staple of both TV and cinema. Some are based on actual events, e.g. *Wolf Hall*, *Chernobyl*, *The Crown*; others are set in the past, but feature fictional or semi-fictional characters, e.g. *Call the Midwife*, *Peaky Blinders*, and *Mad Men*. Interesting periods from the past provide a rich source of inspirational material. Great research will help bring authenticity. These stories need sufficient budgets to cover the costs of set dressing and costumes but this shouldn't put you off at the ideas stage. Examples of features:

- **Selma:** Dr Martin Luther King, Jr.'s march from Selma to Montgomery, Alabama, in 1965, to demand equal voting rights
- **First Man:** a biopic of Neil Armstrong running up to his walk on the Moon on July 20, 1969
- **The Favourite:** in early 18th-century England, a depressed Queen Anne, who's lost her husband and children, is uplifted by a new servant

The first two examples have dramatic events that provide the movie's ending. In *Selma*, it's the dangerous march towards an armed police cordon. In *First Man*, it's when Neil steps from the lunar module to the moon's surface. In *The Favourite*, it's more about what might have happened after the arrival of Abigail into Queen Anne's household. Her lust for improvement drives a wedge between the Queen and her political mouthpiece, Lady Sarah.

As an exercise, pick a historical event that interests you and consider:

- Where should the event appear in the story?
- Is your protagonist linked to it in a meaningful way?
- Does the event change the world?

We'll cover **worlds** in more depth later, but for now, what do I mean by changing the world? It doesn't necessarily mean it affects everyone on earth. In story terms, the protagonist's world can be as small as a room e.g. *The Whale*. In *Selma* and *First Man*, these were history-defining moments. Both are valid.

In writing a historical story, it's up to you how close or not you keep to the truth. Yorgos Lanthimos (director) said of *The Favourite*, 'Some of the things in the film are accurate, and a lot aren't'. You'll likely have to change several things to make it work as an entertaining story. Gaps must be filled, and additional plot twists added. But at this point, as you're just looking for a jumping off point, worry about structure later.

PREMISE

Can you sell the sizzle? How would you pitch the idea for your story in half a sentence? This is not a logline or a tagline. A premise is a neat summation of what is remarkable about your idea. What would make someone raise their eyebrows? For example:

- It's about a schoolgirl who kills monsters (*Buffy*)
- Imagine a boy who can see dead people (*Sixth Sense*)
- A cleaning robot that gets left on an abandoned, dirty Earth falls in love with a sleek robot searching for life (*WALL-E*)

How do you come up with an exciting premise? If previous techniques have failed, try: **what if?** What if? is one of the most potent phrases for brainstorming. It's open, non-judgemental, and can be used repeatedly to keep ideating. What if the moon was made of cheese? Well, it would be *A Grand Day Out* for a cheese-loving inventor and his clever dog if they flew there. What if? is irreverent and fun. It can also be imperative: What if a man could fly? It's the phrase to use as a creative starting point or find a solution if you get stuck. It's versatile too:

- What if you turned that fairground ride into a film?
- What if *Jaws* was set in space?
- What if *Seven Samurai* had happened in the Wild West?

The answers to those three what if? questions are *Pirates of the Caribbean*, *Alien*, and *The Magnificent Seven*. Your first answer to what if? can be as ridiculous as you like too, as you can dial it back on future iterations. But you might find that even the most outlandish ideas have been done. What if a dog grew to the size of a skyscraper? What if the mind of an adult was swapped with someone else/a teenager/a cat? But don't get disheartened. Keep going until you find a premise that inspires you to write.

ANGER IS AN ENERGY

In the song, *Rise*, John Lydon sings, 'Anger is an energy.' He wrote it about apartheid in South Africa and alleged Royal Ulster Constabulary interrogation techniques, such as electric torture. These are serious matters which John wanted to vent about. The song contains the phrase, 'May the road rise with you.' It's an approximate translation of the old Irish blessing: 'go n-éirí an bóthar leat', which is an expression of hope from God that your journey be easy, with no large hills to climb. John wishes the same for those who suffered.

The starting point for your story doesn't have to be as serious as torture. But starting with something that upsets you e.g. injustice, is a good ideator. But equally, it might be that you want to write about innocuous inconveniences e.g. 'I go out to dinner, I wind up with a homework assignment.' (*Curb Your Enthusiasm*). Use what riles you, to inspire you.

CONSTRAINTS

Anything that restricts choice can (counter-intuitively) be helpful in generating ideas. Without constraints it's easy to become paralysed by having too many choices (decision paralysis). Imagine staring at a blank page and being told, 'Write/paint/draw something now!' It can feel overwhelming. But if you introduce some constraints, reducing possible choices, the request becomes more manageable. Like adding a colour wash to a blank canvas. Here are some restrictions to try:

1. Time
2. Location
3. Characters
4. Genre

Ideation.

TIME

Add a temporal limit to your story idea. Perhaps the story must begin and finish in one week, day, or hour. Might the story run in real-time? Could it run backwards. We accept that stories are edited with the boring bits cut out e.g. the protagonist brushing their teeth, going to the toilet or eating. Time can even become part of the premise, particularly in sci-fi e.g. *Timecrimes*, *Primer*, *Deathloop*, *Edge of Tomorrow*, and *Beyond the Infinite Two Minutes*, all use a causal loop phenomenon to put their characters into more and more absurd situations. Often when they try to correct mistakes made in previous loops; they stir up more trouble for later.

LOCATION

The physical setting can be a useful constraint. Agatha Christie liked single locations for her stories, e.g. *Murder on the Nile* and *The Orient Express*, to trap her suspects and create a pressure cooker. This technique is invaluable for low-budget filmmaking as moving between locations eats up lots of time. In 2021, Bristol Council gave my film club access to Ashton Court Mansion for a month. We made a dozen films with a 10-person crew. It was big enough to have plenty of variety and we could store kit overnight. Single location stories are popular in horror or sci-fi:

- **Frozen:** three friends find themselves trapped on a ski lift chair
- **Cube:** strangers wake in separate, but interconnected cells, of a massive cube
- **Dogtooth:** is set in a compound in which parents will not let their children leave

A single location helps to keep the budget down, but this doesn't mean it has to be a low-budget indie, e.g. *The Shining*,

Panic Room, Knives Out, or *The Cabin in the Woods*. Another advantage of using location as a constraint is that you might have access to somewhere interesting, as we did.

CHARACTERS

You can reduce choice by limiting the number of characters. While particularly useful for novels, it's also good for features, making the story easier to follow. And for low budget filmmaking, cheaper too. If there are too many characters, we may struggle to remember who's who. Keeping the number of characters to less than a dozen can help. And if someone is reading your screenplay, you don't want them to have to juggle too many characters in their head. As the number of characters reduces, you also give them more *screen time*. This may help to attract a higher calibre of actor. Films like *The Father*, *Memento*, or *The Room*, give their leads plenty of time to shine.

GENRE

Start with a genre. Skip back to the section on genre for a refresh.

By adding constraints, you can stimulate creativity. Using limitations is a common technique in poetry e.g. using a particular verse form, only one vowel, or not using a certain letter. But it can be applied to other forms. For example, *Gadsby* by Ernest Vincent Wright, self-published in 1939, is a novel without the letter 'e'. In *Lemons Lemons Lemons Lemons Lemons*, the characters' speech is limited to 140 characters.

Others have used constraints in more physical ways. Dogme 95 was a filmmaking movement started in 1995 by the Danish directors Lars von Trier and Thomas Vinterberg. They created the Vows of Chastity, rules by which a film must be made to be accredited as a Dogme 95. These included:

1. Shooting must be done on location
2. No props and sets
3. The sound must never be produced apart from the images or vice versa
4. The camera must be hand-held. Any movement or immobility attainable in hand is permitted
5. Optical work and filters are forbidden

Thirty-one films were made that met the criteria before Dogme 95 stopped its verification.

READ A NEWSPAPER

An exercise popular in writing workshops involves reading newspapers. Attendees flick through them until a story piques their interest – imagine your subconscious raising a hand at the back of the classroom. The section is cut out or transcribed. Try it yourself now, I'll wait. Right, can you determine the following:

1. The main character?
2. Where they are?
3. Is it better as a TV show or a film?

Like any ideation technique, repeat until you have something you want to continue with.

FIND AN IMAGE

Images can be an effective trigger for ideas. This particular method works best with pictures you've not seen before. Perhaps an art book that's a collection of paintings or photographs. And like the newspaper exercise, casually glide through it until an image intrigues you enough to stop. Perhaps it's a stunning landscape scene? Or a mother holding their child? Whatever resonates with you is valid. Now, interrogate the picture. Are there multiple characters in the image? If so, what connects them? Are they family, or do they share an interest? If it's a picture without characters, where is it? Who might have just left the scene, or who is about to enter it? If you don't have a suitable book, use a search engine. Use a word that might be a topic you want to explore, e.g. jealousy, cheerleading, revenge, and search until you find a spark.

OBJECTS

In much the same way as the two methods above, you can use physical objects to find inspiration. You could gather a dozen cheap objects from a charity shop. Ones that fit in the palm of your hand are best. Find a space to work and lay them out in front of you. Pick one that appeals. Place it in front of you and write down any thoughts it triggers.

SHAPING

Now that you have an idea, you need to shape so it starts to resemble a story. In this section, I'll go through some techniques to help do that.

RESEARCH

Research, or as some might call it, procrastination, is a great method for moulding your idea into a story. For those of us who enjoy research, it's tempting to stay here for a long time. For those that hate it, it can feel like torture. How much time you spend on it is up to you. If you don't know much about your subject matter, you'll have to put the hours in. Luckily, we have the internet to research anything from historical events, to niche hobbies, to famous people, to obscure laws, to archaic medical procedures.

A good idea when starting your research is to create a space to save material. This could be as simple as a text document with copied and pasted material. Or specialised software like *Evernote* or *OneNote*. Or just write in a notebook. Whatever you use, cataloguing the material will prove itself later. Although the internet is a convenient resource, don't discount textbooks or libraries. A powerful method is to interview. Someone affected by the events of your story, the actual person your story's based on, or familiar with the world you're creating. Daragh Carville, writing *The Bay*, spoke to several Family Liaison Officers and what they told him reassured him that a TV series could be based on their profession.

ELEMENTS OF CIRCUMSTANCE

The Elements of Circumstance, or Kipling's Questions, is a quick way to query your idea. Initially proposed by Aristotle, each 'W' helps expand your idea. The Elements of Circumstance are:

- **Who?**
- **What?**
- **Where?**
- **When?**
- **Why?**

Using the film, *Coda*, a set of questions and answers could look like this:

1. Who is the lead character? Answer: Ruby
2. What does she want? Answer: to leave home and study music
3. Where is it set? Answer: a coastal fishing town in the USA
4. When does it occur? Answer: it's contemporary
5. Why should we care about her? Answer: she's the only speaking person in a deaf family

To the existing Ws, **how** can be added. For *Coda*, this could be:

6. How does the story play out? Answer: Ruby convinces them to let her go

As well as being a valuable way of interrogating your idea, the Elements of Circumstance can also be used to structure a treatment or a pitch. If you do use it for that purpose, you might also want to answer two more questions:

Ideation.

1. Why do you want to tell this story?
2. Why is now the right time for this story?

It's okay if you don't have answers to all the Elements of Circumstance, as any answers will help shape your story.

LOGLINE

A quick method of judging a story's strength is its logline.[2] This is usually a single, long sentence that summarises your story. A well-written logline describes who the story is about, what they want and the challenges they face. A logline has become a fast method of gauging the appeal of a story, particularly when pitching it. This doesn't mean that a bad reaction to your logline should stop you writing. But it's better to know something may need fixing now rather than later. There is no absolute consensus on logline format, but I'll suggest a couple of options. The first and most simple:

Protagonist + Inciting Incident + Protagonist's Goal + Central Conflict

For *The Wizard of Oz*, this could be: 'A farm girl is swept away by a tornado to a strange, dangerous land and to return home must find a powerful wizard which means following a yellow brick road'. My logline has told us who the story is about, what threw them off course, what they want, and why achieving it won't be easy.

We can go further:

---

2. A logline was a navigational tool used on ships that consisted of a yarn of weighted string. When dragged behind a vessel, the number of visible weights indicated the travel speed.

In a Setting, a Flawed Protagonist has a Problem caused by an Antagonist and faces Conflict as they try to achieve a Goal.

If I use *Rear Window*, 'In Greenwich Village, a nosey photographer thinks he's caught a neighbour committing murder, but no one believes him.'

You can have more than one protagonist or antagonist. For *Ocean's Eleven*: 'In Las Vegas, an ex-con forms a team to rob three casinos owned by the man dating his ex-girlfriend.' Or *Avengers: Infinity War*, 'Too weak individually, the Avengers band together to stop a mad titan from controlling six superpower-giving jewels.'

You can also include the emotional journey of the protagonist in a logline. Using *Kramer vs Kramer*: 'In Manhattan, a work-obsessed husband fights for sole custody of his child, but realises that his son's welfare is more important than winning'. A good logline provides a handy means of communicating your idea to others (and is a useful reference for yourself).

How long should a logline be? What's the magic number? Is there one? Some feel it's 24, others that it's 26. In the loglines above, the word counts are 29, 18, 19, 17 and 23. By no means have I been consistent. The average word count is 21. My target word count when I'm writing loglines is 24. Find your own sweet spot or start with mine.

SCULPTING

I've called this next phase, Sculpting. At this point, you've got some or all of a premise, a protagonist, the time they live in, where they are, what they want, and what's going to prevent them from getting it. But although these are vital elements, for most, it's still a long way from having sufficient material to start writing. For others, it may be enough. But for those that need greater definition, let's create a **skeleton document**.

SKELETON DOCUMENT

A skeleton document records your story's framework – the bones holding it together. It's a temporal list of the most significant parts. Details aren't required. With it, you can check you've enough supporting structure to support a long form story. My skeleton document is protagonist-centric and is focussed on external events. It's split into a conventional 3-Act structure and is based on the Hero's Journey by Joseph Campbell (more on that later). Each element needs no more than a single-sentence response. As well as helping to develop your own stories, it can be used to analyse others. For instance, you could fill it in as you watch a film.

Act 1

Protagonist: ....
Home World: ....
Want: ....
Flaw: ....
Need: ....
Antagonist: ....
Inciting Incident: ....
Objective: ....

Act 2

Alien World: ....
Mentor: ....
Friends: ....
Obstacles: ....
Midpoint: ....
Obstacles: ....
Objective: ....

Act 3

Shadow World: ....
Final Fight: ....
Failure: ....
Resurrection: ....
All or Nothing: ....
Success or Failure: ....
Resolution: ....

Figure 2: The Skeleton Document.

Let's use the film *A Few Good Men*, by Aaron Sorkin, to see what a completed one looks like:

Act 1

Protagonist: Kaffe recently graduated from Harvard and is a Navy lawyer and officer

Home World: enjoys playing softball

Wants: to avoid going to court, so always settles out of it

Flaw: coward

Inner Need: to step out of his father's shadow, a famous trial lawyer

Antagonist: Jessup, the commanding officer at Guantanamo Bay

Inciting Incident: Kaffe is assigned to defend two marines (Dawson and Downey) accused of murdering another soldier, Santiago, at Guantanamo Bay

Objective: to get them a minimal jail term without going to court

Act 2

Alien World: Guantanamo Bay

Mentor: none

Friends: Lt. Cdr. JoAnne Galloway

Obstacles: getting the transfer order, JoAnne becomes Downey's counsel and Matthew Markinson, Jessup's subordinate, disappears

Midpoint: Dawson and Downey won't plead guilty. Kaffe is called a coward

Obstacles: Kaffe's never been in court, and can't prove the doctor lied

Objective: to prove something can be a rule even if it's not a regulation

Act 3

Shadow World: a courtroom

Final Fight: Kaffe wants to convince the court that Jessup is a liar

Failure: the transfer record for Santiago was correct. Markinson is found dead

All or Nothing: Kaffe puts Jessup on the stand, risking his career. He outsmarts Jessup

Success or Failure: Jessup admits he allowed his men to rough up Santiago

Resolution: Jessup's arrested. Dawson and Downey are found not guilty of murder but are dishonourably discharged. Kaffe helps them to realise they can have honour even if they're not soldiers. Dawson salutes Kaffe

The completed skeleton document provides an overview of the story with minimum descriptive elements and no dialogue.

Figure 3: Objectives.

OBJECTIVES

Objectives help to describe how your protagonist's want is transformed into something tangible and near term (Figure 3). Luke (*Star Wars: Episode IV: A New Hope*) wants adventure and he can get it if he returns the droids to Princess Leia (Super Objective). To achieve this, he has some intermediate objectives. He must find Obi-Wan Kenobi, reach Alderaan, and so on. He may or may not be achieve them. But with each success or failure, he's having an adventure. Objectives are a common tool used by actors to navigate scenes. They help them understand their character's short term desires while also being aware of their ultimate target.

OUTLINE

An outline is a prose document summarising your story. It should include all your key characters and scenes. It can vary from a couple of pages to as many as to 30 to 40. It's similar to a treatment, although those normally include images. For a feature, most outlines are five to 15 pages. Outlines tend to be written in a dry, factual manner, but you can include character names and descriptions – even snippets of dialogue. As a document, it should be recognisable as a story, with a clear path for your main protagonist from beginning to end. This document can often be one of the final documents you complete before you start your script.

CHARACTER DESCRIPTIONS

For most audiences, characters make a story. The audience will forgive a plot with as many holes as a fishing net or flooded with on-the-nose dialogue[3] if it has a mesmerising protagonist and

---

3. Dialogue that states the obvious e.g. information that is known, or lacks subtlety.

strong secondary characters. I'll focus on **character** later, but if you've been following the book in order, now is a good point to flesh them out a bit. A few bullet points or a paragraph of text describing who they are, what motivates them, their flaws, quirks, or distinctive behaviours, is a valuable resource be able to refer to later. Write each one in proportion to their importance to the story. So, the protagonist might get a paragraph, whereas a bit part character only needs a sentence.

PLOT TABLE

A plot table (Table 1) is a functional way to record and develop your story's plot points. Like a turning point, a plot point is a significant event that changes the protagonist's knowledge or progress towards an objective or their ultimate goal. A plot point is often a significant action taken by the protagonist or antagonist or a twist in the story, such as a betrayal or unexpected information surfacing. Your plot table can have as many rows as needed, and you could add or remove columns. In my version, I've 10 rows (enough for a feature) and six columns. You only need to add a small amount of detail for each cell. The primary purpose of the plot table is to make sure there's *enough* plot. And that the main characters are **actively** involved.

In the second column, you add the plot point. The third, fourth, and fifth columns signify who the event is most associated with some text or a tick or cross. In some cases, neither the protagonist nor the antagonist might be involved, so you use column 5. In column 6, record how it **advances** the story. It should, even if it sends the protagonist **backwards**. Plot points should be meaningful rather than just being exciting. I do allow myself one random plot point – the unexpected life event (ULE). In many ways, stories are more predictable than real life.

PLOT POINT	ACTION / DECISION / NEW INFO	PROTAGONIST	ANTAGONIST	OTHER	HOW DOES IT ADVANCE THE PLOT?
1.					
2.					
3.					
4.					
5.					
6.					
7.					
8.					
9.					
10.					

Table 1: Plot Table.

SEQUENCES

Sequences are an ordered list of events that happen in a scene. Like a condensed version of the skeleton document, they're a handy structural tool. However, the terms I've used are deliberately different to create clear water. Sequences ensure you've a character with an objective (a **want**), that they do something to try to achieve it (**do**), and there's an outcome (**get**). The 8-step sequence can be used multiple times to develop your story. Here it is:

1. Current situation
2. Trigger event
3. Character's objective
4. Character's options
5. Choice taken
6. Interaction
7. Result
8. New situation

Let's go through each one.

CURRENT SITUATION

The current situation (1) is the setting for your new scene; the physical surroundings and your character's state within it. It might be an easily recognisable location, e.g. living room, prairie, swimming pool, but it can be anything. And using the latter example, is your character drowning or lying on a lilo? The character can be whoever is the Point of View (POV) for the scene. So if we've a missing cat, and our protagonist is searching for it, they may have followed the sound of meowing to a tree.

TRIGGER EVENT

This step is the event that activates the scene. Like an Inciting Incident, the trigger event catalyses what unfolds next. It usually occurs at the start, but could be pre-scene. If, for instance, our character was sent across space to land in a pit of snakes, the trigger event didn't strictly occur in this scene. A trigger event pre-scene provides a narrative flow and is ideal for switches between time and space. The surprise must be created when the trigger event is in the scene. For example, the end of each episode of the original *Quantum Leap*, when Sam finds himself in a new time, place, and body.

CHARACTER'S OBJECTIVE

You now need a character to react to the trigger event. If it's the pit of snakes, it might simply be to get out without being bitten. In most cases, the protagonist has arrived in the current situation with an objective e.g. find the cat, but the trigger event – the cat's in the tree – means they've a problem to solve. Dorothy, in the *Wizard of Oz*, has a short-term objective to speak to the wizard in the Emerald Castle, with her ultimate goal to return home.

CHARACTER'S OPTIONS

Faced with the change of circumstances caused by the trigger event, our character has a new objective e.g. get the cat out of the tree. So they need to choose what to do to achieve it. Their choice should reveal something about themselves and affect their chance of success. They have three categories of options: **persuade**, **fight**, or **seduce**. It's a good idea to consider several alternatives and write them down. So, if our hero wants to enter a night club, but discovers its full and blocked by a bouncer, what might they do? They could give them a bribe (persuade), they could knock them out (fight), or they could offer them sex (seduce).

All the options offer some flexibility. For instance, fight could be non-physical e.g. when David faces the Shadow King in *Legion* or the wine-drinking scene in *The Princess Bride*. It's reported that each scene of *Game of Thrones* was written as fight, whatever the scenario. In *A Portrait of a Woman on Fire*, Celine Sciama choose desire, similar to option 3, to drive her scenes. Our character could also choose to flee or even surrender. It's still an active choice, not to fight.

CHOICE TAKEN

Once you've decided what approach your character takes, summarise it. So, if our hero has chosen to **persuade** the cat in the tree to come down, record an option or two e.g. call its name or place food on the ground. If they've chosen **fight**, they might use a ladder to climb the tree and grab it. Check that their choice fits with the character's personality, the genre, and their emotional state. For example, if it's a slapstick film, they might bounce on a trampoline to snatch it.

INTERACTION

When your character acts on their chosen strategy, they enter an exchange with something or someone else. If the hero chose to put food on the ground for the cat, did the cat come down? Or did it climb higher? The Interaction should be entertaining, surprising, or informative; otherwise, why have it? As Alfred Hitchcock said, 'What is drama but life with the dull bits cut out.'

RESULT

Following the Interaction, they'll be a result. Did your character get the cat? Or did it run down their back, onto the ladder, then scamper away? The most satisfying results are unexpected or hard-won. You'll lose your audience if your story's full of predictable scenes. You need unexpected outcomes. Perhaps calling the cat, or offering food failed, but shaking the tree brought it down into their arms.

NEW SITUATION

Following the outcome of our character's chosen approach, how has the situation changed? Perhaps the cat is so high up the tree that the ladder can't reach it. Or did the character get the cat, with a scratch for good measure? The outcomes often fall within one of four categories:

1. Physical
2. Emotional
3. Societal
4. Knowledge

Using the cat in the tree example, here are four possible outcomes:

- **Physical:** the cat is safe, but the tree had to be cut down to get it
- **Emotional:** the cat's dead and its owner distraught
- **Societal:** the cat turns into a human, revealing the existence of shapeshifters
- **Knowledge:** the cat's rescued, but it's not the missing cat

A comprehensive set of sequences is similar to a set of beat cards.[4] You can even print a simplified sequence onto an index card and fill them in. On completion, sequences allow you to review your story quickly. For instance, you could check how frequently a character appears or how easily your protagonist achieves their objectives or whether you've a variety of outcomes of if they keep using the same approach. If you decide to write your sequences on index cards, it can help to have a simplified format for each step:

1. Start
2. Trigger
3. Want
4. Options
5. Do
6. Interaction
7. Get
8. End

I'll now use Sequences on two scenes.

---

4. Also called index or note cards, they are neat way to organise a story as they can be moved, edited, and replaced quickly. Each one can summarise a scene, event, or a beat.

The Power of the Dog

The film is about Phil Burbank, a closeted homosexual cowboy whose excessive machismo contributes to his death. The scene I'll examine occurs after Phil has been mean to the son of a widowed restaurateur, Rose. Phil's brother, George, checks in on Rose and finds her in tears. George returns to the bedroom he shares with his brother.

1. **Current Situation:** Phil and George's bedroom at night
2. **Trigger Event:** Phil's behaviour in the restaurant. Phil asks George where he's been
3. **Character's Objective:** George wants Phil to admit he was rude
4. **Character's Options (Persuade, Fight or Seduce):** seduction isn't an option as they're brothers. George could drag Phil to Rose to apologise but he's too timid. George could sleep elsewhere
5. **Choice Taken:** George chooses persuasion
6. **Interaction:** George tells Phil what he did wrong. Phil disagrees
7. **Result:** George gets into bed and they don't speak
8. **New Situation:** George holds a grudge against his brother

George knows that he could never win against Phil in a physical altercation, even a verbal exchange. But he might just persuade him to realise he was in the wrong. The POV is mostly with Phil, who initiates the scene. Phil's refusal to accept any fault leaves George hurt. The situation has changed, although you don't see the repercussions till later. They may be sleeping next to each other, but there's now a chasm between them.

Better Call Saul

Better Call Saul is a prequel series to *Breaking Bad* and focuses on the lawyer James (Jimmy) McGill. This scene occurs just after Jimmy fails to secure a client for his new law practice.

1. **Current Situation:** Jimmy, on the phone, drives his Suzuki Esteem through suburbia
2. **Trigger Event:** a skateboarder bounces off his windscreen. Jimmy stops. The uninjured brother threatens to call the police
3. **Character's Objective:** Jimmy wants to help the injured skater but doesn't want the police involved
4. **Character's Options (Persuade, Fight or Seduce):** Jimmy could drive off but it's not in his nature. He wouldn't win in a fight, so he chooses persuasion
5. **Choice Taken:** Jimmy asks them not to call the police
6. **Interaction:** the skateboarders will comply if Jimmy pays them. Jimmy realises it's a scam and threatens them
7. **Result:** the skateboarders run off
8. **New Situation:** Jimmy's left with a broken windshield

This scene is an excellent insight into Jimmy's character early on in the series. Jimmy is seen as careless – driving at speed while on the phone. But he stops the car, as he's concerned for the skater. We discover that Jimmy's smart when he sees through their con. His rebellious nature and willingness to bend the rules become a strength here. The skateboarders being fakers gives the scene an entertaining and unexpected twist.

WAYPOINTS

If you're someone who's keen to just dive in, there's nothing wrong with writing a few scenes, moments, or beats. Perhaps it's a situation or an image that's been the spark. We can use these snippets as waypoints. Whether they stay in the final script doesn't matter. It's words on the page. From my experience it will likely involve your protagonist and a life-changing moment. Celine Sciamma writes a few key scenes to provide herself with a visual journey through her story. I find that characters and plot emerge together. A great character is just a mannequin if given nothing to do. A plot is an empty sports field without players. Put some flags in the ground.

SCENE SHEET

A scene (or beat) sheet is a table or list recording the significant moments of your story. A scene is defined by a change of time or location. A beat is smaller, like a heartbeat, a hit on a drum, or the end of an *Eastenders* episode. It can be an emotional moment or a revelation. You can have more than one beat in a scene. Paul Schrader uses scene sheets, (although he calls them outlines) and defines each as, 'A list of everything that happens.' It's the final part of his process before he writes the script. He begins with a problem faced by a character, elevates it to a metaphor for life (the theme), describes the plot, then shapes the story through verbal telling before producing a scene sheet.

Schrader's scene sheet is a tabulated, ordered list of about 50 scenes written as sentences. These form two columns with around 30 lines in the first column. He also estimates how many script pages each scene will become when written. If a scene is one to two pages on average, he'll get close to a full-length script. In Table 2, you can see a version based on his template.

I've altered it to make it more symmetrical, with the midpoint at the bottom. You'll see a further iteration in the Structure section, providing even greater utility.

#	SCENE	#	SCENE
1		29	
2		30	
3		31	
4		32	
5		33	
6		34	
7		35	
8		36	
9		37	
10		38	
11		39	
12		40	
13		41	
14		42	
15		43	
16		44	
17		45	
18		46	
19		47	
20		48	
21		49	
22		50	
23		51	
24		52	
25		53	
26		54	
27		55	
28		56	

Table 2: Scene Sheet.

CARDING

Beat cards are a well known screenwriting tool. Each index card (or sticky note) summarises a beat or a scene. Cards vary in format but usually include the location, a character, and what they do next. They're easy to write, are shuffleable and can be laid flat or stuck to a board. There's even software versions. There's no agreed number of cards you should have for a feature, but it's usually at least 50. You can use different colours e.g. for different characters or each Act. What you write on each card is up to you, but here's some suggestions:

- A number (so you can order them)
- The setting e.g. where are we, or what time of day is
- The situation our character finds themselves in
- What happens?
- Which characters are in it?
- What does the scene reveal to the audience? For example, does it:
  - Introduce a new character
  - Is there a plot twist?
  - Provide new information
  - Reveal something about a character
  - What do they want?
  - How do they feel?
  - Their flaw
  - An emotional temperature check for your protagonist

For the last element, you could record whether they're upbeat, sad, or reflective. You could use valences, e.g. +, - for this, or smiley faces. The added benefit is as a continuity check between scenes. For example, it's unlikely you'd go from a scene where the protagonist is devastated by the death of someone to laughing at a party. My version (Figure 4) is opposite.

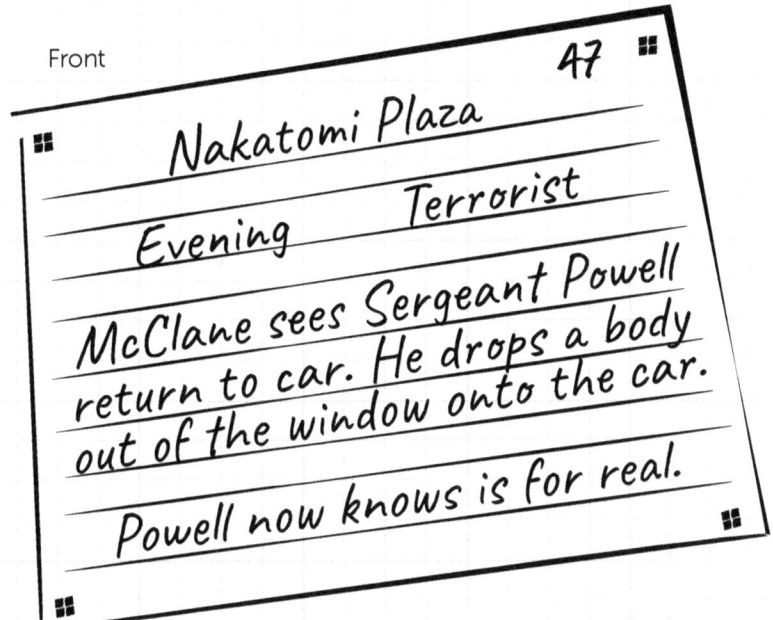

Figure 4: Beat or Scene Cards.

ORAL TELLING

Blake Snyder used to stand in coffee queues and pitch people his latest script idea. If they showed interest, he knew he was on the right track. If they're interest dipped, he realised more work was needed. If you're too afraid to talk to people in queues, pitch it to friends or a writer's group. Or read the story aloud to yourself or have your computer read it to you. Listening to our words can help spot things that reading silently can't.

WORKFLOW

A workflow is a series of steps that form a process to complete a task. In our case, it's the combination and order of pre-scriptwriting techniques. Hopefully, at this point you've a set of techniques that work for you. Here's an example of one of my workflows:

1. Your character or a situation
2. A logline
3. A skeleton document
4. An outline
5. Cards

You might want different workflows for different projects, e.g. a short film may need fewer steps than a feature film. Try different combinations. A good workflow should get you to the point at which you can write your first draft. As you do so, its theme, if not already identified, should be revealed.

THEME

The theme is the *soul* of your story. It can be a word, moral, statement, argument, or question. It's what's left if you remove character and plot. Sometimes ethereal, it can add depth and memorability to your story. In your chosen workflow, it's usually best to let it emerge, rather than start with it. Doing this roots your story in character and avoids them being a mouthpiece for an authorial opinion. But you can start with theme, after all, *there are no rules*. Theme is something that can resonate with its audience long after they've left the cinema or closed a book. Theme adds depth and meaning. It can hold a TV series together or be used to bring variety to sitcom episodes. There can also be more than one. Let's look at some examples. I've included the premise for context.

The Big Bang Theory

- **Premise:** three quirky male scientists/engineers desperate for girlfriends and one who isn't
- **Theme:** can nerds find love?

Dad's Army

- **Premise:** the adventures of a British Home Guard
- **Theme:** how a group of men from different classes and backgrounds pull together despite having an incompetent leader

Everything Everywhere All at Once

- **Premise:** a hard-working mother finds herself jumping between universes to prevent her daughter from destroying everything
- **Themes:** family, acceptance, existentialism, sacrifice, nihilism

If you look at the themes at play in the examples above, you can see how many of them are familiar: love, bad bosses, family dynamics. Their universality gives those shows a greater chance of resonating with a larger audience. *The Big Bang Theory* is like *The L Word*, *Friends*, or *Queer as Folk*, in that it's mostly about single people searching for a partner. Therefore most of the action occurs outside the workplace. It's the same for *Dad's Army*. The platoon's experience reflects many people's experiences of working life (or being in a sports team). You have a boss (or coach), rules to follow, and work with people you may not get on with. *The Office* is another example.

A theme can help shape your story through its relationship to your characters. To do this, let each character have a different take on it. This will help to generate distinct characters and more opportunities for conflict between them. And the greater variety of characters gives your audience a broader range of viewers to align with. Let's look at the characters in *The Big Bang Theory*, and their relationship to the theme. Formatting theme as a **question** makes this method work better.

CAN NERDS FIND LOVE?

- **Sheldon:** yes, but he isn't looking for it
- **Leonard:** yes, he has an on-off relationship with Penny
- **Howard:** yes, when he finds someone like his mother
- **Rajesh:** no, as he keeps messing things up

Whether the writers used a theme to define the characters doesn't matter. What's important is that's its a technique *you* can use to achieve similar results. The simplest way of describing your theme is a **single word**. This may not always be possible or easy, but it's worth trying. Here's some examples:

- **Spider-Man: No Way Home:** failure
- **Finding Nemo:** trust
- **Jaws:** water
- **The Power of the Dog:** masculinity

Although all protagonists fail as they pursue their objective(s), perhaps none fails as spectacularly and as often as Peter Parker. But he's a teenager, given extraordinary powers, so it's hardly surprising. But if you look the other main characters in *Spider-Man: No Way Home*, they also had a strong relationship with failure:

- **Otto Octavius:** failed to save his wife
- **Norman Osbourne:** failed as a business leader and father
- **Curt Connors:** failed as a scientist
- **Maxwell Dillon:** failed to be seen
- **Dr Strange:** failed to become the Sorcerer Supreme

Each character is given a chance at redemption, to atone for their failures. And they're helped by three versions of Spider-Man, all trying to do better. Even Norman Osborne tries at first.

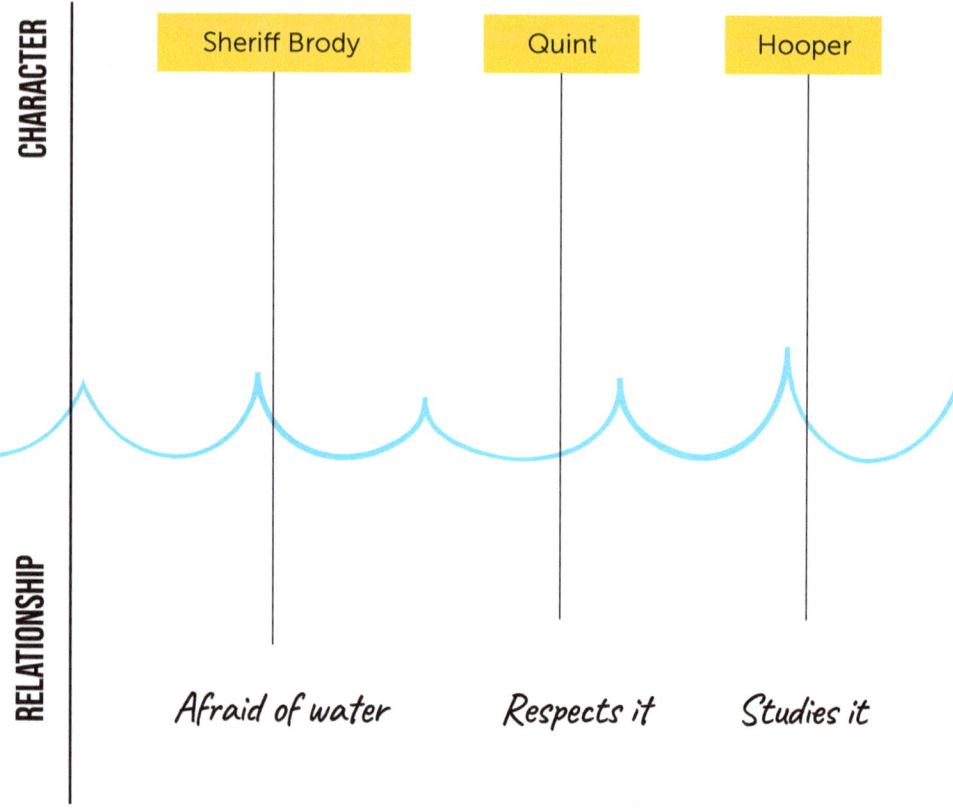

Figure 5: Characters in *Jaws* Thematic Relationship to Water.

What about *Jaws*? Let's look at the relationships of the main characters to water (Figure 5). The mayor wants to keep the beach open, whereas Brody wants it shut. Hooper wants to study the shark; Quint intends to kill it. These different viewpoints represent a diverse range of opinions. This allows an audience to participate, deciding which point of view they most agree with. Is the shark doing anything wrong? The ocean is its home, which we've entered. Using theme in this way also helps us to check that the protagonist and antagonist are in **opposition**. In *Jaws*, Brody hates water while the shark revels in it.

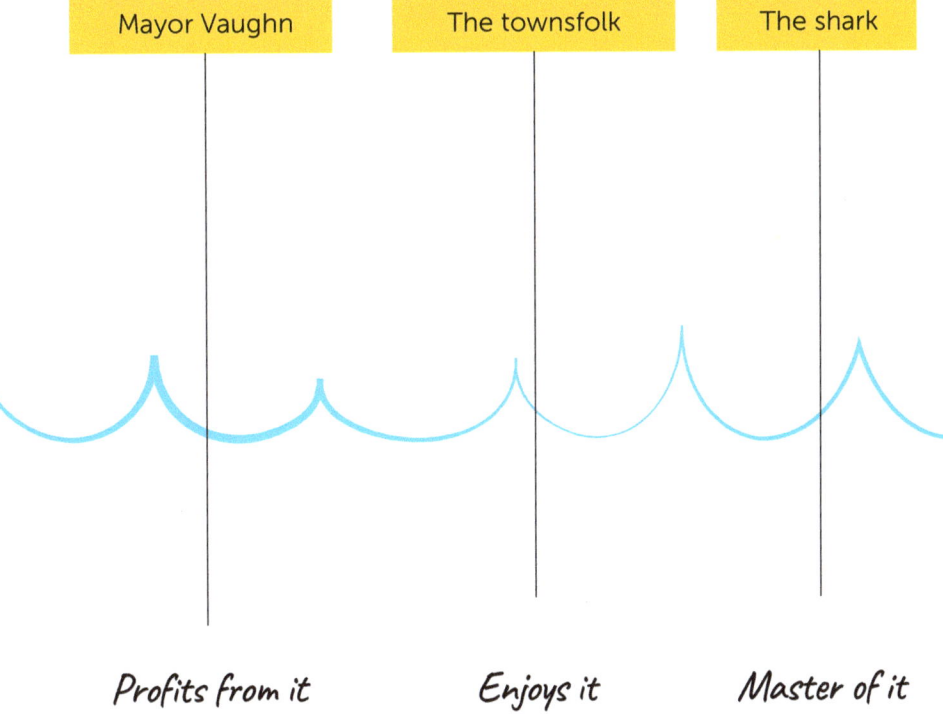

Theme should influence the tone, pitch, and as you've seen, the characters of your story. Theme can be related to your character's misbelief (created from their flaw) which I'll cover later. This can be particularly helpful in tying together your main characters with the theme, and each other. If you write your theme as an **objectively true statement**, the protagonist's belief should contradict it. So for *Jaws*, it might be, 'Water is safe'. Some other examples:

Aftersun

- **Theme:** no parent is perfect
- **Misbelief:** Calum believes he's not a good father

Aftersun is about a father, living abroad, visited by his daughter. It's mostly a two-hander and covers what we gather to be the last time the two of them spend together. Calum is deeply troubled, possibly through acute ADHD, and at times, derelict in his parenting duties. His daughter is mostly unperturbed by this and loves him unconditionally. As an adult, you get glimpses of her, reminiscing about the best holiday she'd ever had. The rug he bought on their last holiday lies at the foot of her bed.

Midnight Mass

- **Theme:** religion is a belief-based system not a rules-based one
- **Misbelief:** Riley believes that since he's alive, and no religion can give him a satisfactory reason why he should be, there are no gods

Midnight Mass is about belief. Riley doesn't believe in any god, as what god would allow him to live, while his innocent passenger died, due to his careless driving. Father Paul believes the vampire is an angel, a mistaken belief based on his diminished mental state when they meet for the first time. Erin does believe in God and, at her death, believes that she will live on, if not in heaven, in the stars.

ASSOCIATIONS

A single, thematic word can be used to create associations with other words. These new words might help develop your story. They can be anything, but a noun or verb works best. They might relate to the tone or genre of your movie e.g. revenge, love, or shotgun. But equally they might offer nothing useful at all. Try this method by hand, using a large piece of paper — A4 or bigger. Let's try one using the word, book (Figure 6).

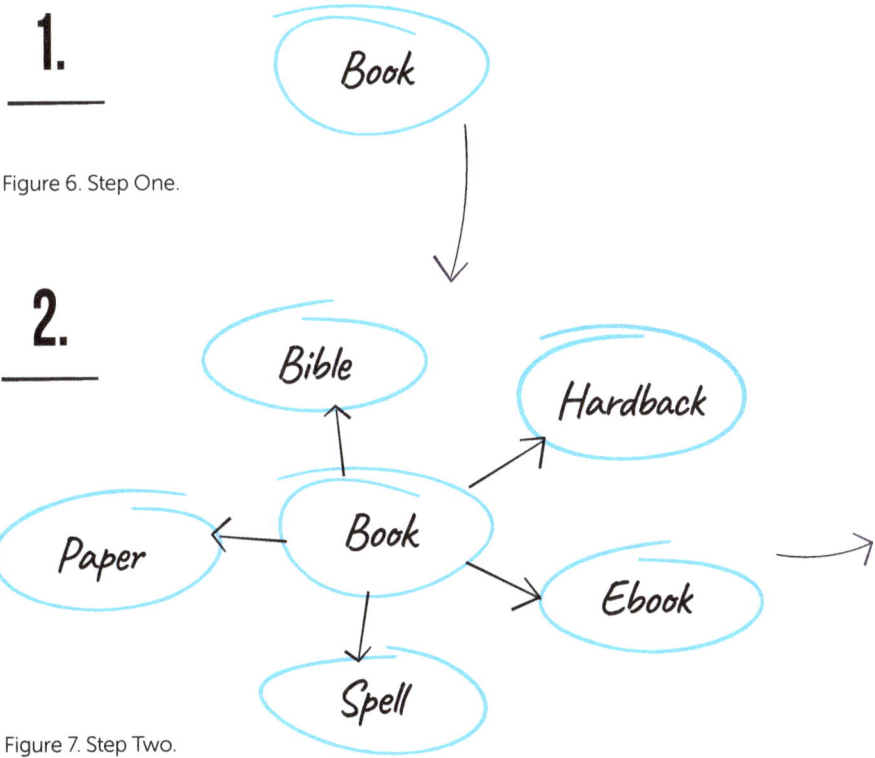

Figure 6. Step One.

Figure 7. Step Two.

Go further, by adding words to the outer ring (Figure 8).

3.

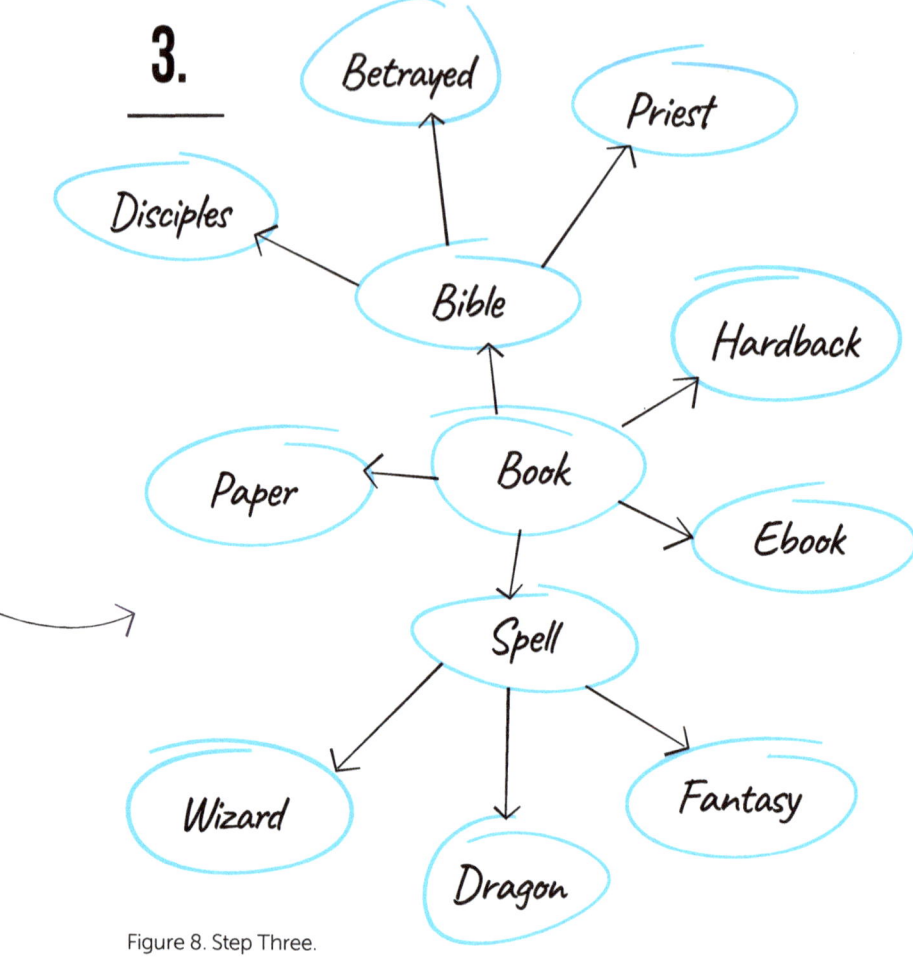

Figure 8. Step Three.

This final diagram should expose areas of interest, perhaps even scene ideas. You might find a node you want to use as a new starting point on a new page. The entire word list(s) is now a resource. It's worth having to hand when you write your script as it can act like a story-specific vocabulary. For example, you might have used the word **money** several times in the action lines and want to find an alternative. Or you could use a synonym in a line of dialogue if you want to add subtext. For example, if your story is about equal pay, instead of saying, 'It's not something to fight about', instead write, 'It's not something to **wage** war over.'

Sometimes single words aren't enough. We can expand on this association method to include phrases, such as aphorisms or idioms. For instance, if your thematic word was *money*, you might write in a new node:

- Dirty money
- Money is no object
- Money is the root of all evil

TRANSFORMATIONS

In this technique devised by Robert McKee, you take your thematic word and transform it to increasingly negative extremes of its meaning. The resulting three words can help define Acts 1, 2, and 3. Here are the three steps:

1. What is the opposite of the thematic word?
2. What is a worse word than your new word?
3. What is an even worse word than that new word?

Let's use *Willy Wonka and the Chocolate Factory* to illustrate his method. The premise is that children from around the world are given the opportunity to visit the mysterious chocolate factory. The audience slowly realise that Wonka is testing them. He wants to know who he can trust with his legacy. So, let's use **trust** as our thematic word:

1. Opposite of trust ⟶ distrust
2. Worse than distrust ⟶ suspicion
3. Worse than suspicion ⟶ betrayal

If we take the three words: distrust, suspicion, and betrayal, we find that they neatly describe Wonka's state of mind through the film's three Acts. Initially, Wonka distrusts everyone, believing they're all out to steal the recipes for his sweets. So, he becomes a recluse. But Wonka wants to pass on his business to someone else, so he runs a competition, based on luck, to create a shortlist of successors. However, most of the children and their parents manipulate the game to increase their chances of finding a golden ticket. He gets his shortlist, including Charlie.

In Act 2, Wonka takes them on a factory tour but he's suspicious of their real intentions. In Act 3, the remaining children are gifted a new, everlasting gobstopper. All but one sells it, betraying his trust. The one that doesn't, Charlie, is given the keys to the castle.

Aristotle

Now seems the right time to talk about Aristotle. He was a philosopher and teacher who wrote *Poetics*, the first book on writing and the one Aaron Sorkin stated contains all you need to know.

One of Aristotle's observations aligns with Mckee's method. Aristotle suggested structuring a 3-Act story as a philosophical argument. In Act 1, you present your **hypothesis** – a belief system employed by your protagonist, which mostly works for them. In Act 2, they're confronted with an opposing belief system by the antagonist (**antithesis**). This makes them doubt themselves, but they reject the alternative and carry on. Finally, in Act 3, the two-belief systems clash again, and this time the protagonist modifies their belief system by **synthesising** a new one that incorporates elements of their antagonist's. Let's see some examples:

The Matrix

- **Hypothesis:** the world is as it seems
- **Antithesis:** the real world is hidden
- **Synthesis:** a person can exist in both worlds

1917

- **Hypothesis:** even in trench warfare an infantry soldier can make a difference
- **Antithesis:** war is fought by generals in tents
- **Synthesis:** an infantry soldier, allowed to leave the trenches, can save many lives

Promising Young Woman

- **Hypothesis:** privileged men can be brought to justice
- **Antithesis:** privileged men escape justice
- **Synthesis:** privileged men can be brought to justice but women will pay a high personal cost

All the protagonists in these films suffer to reach their goals. Like mythical heroes, they have to make a significant sacrifice to **save the world**. Aristotle's system provides a simple, 3-stage framework for your story, using the opposing belief systems of the protagonist and antagonist.

PROTAGONIST VS ANTAGONIST

I've shown how opposing belief systems can provide a structure to a story. Those beliefs are most associated with the protagonist and antagonist. If we convert their beliefs into *wants*, we can move from something ephemeral into something more practical. Here's some examples:

James Bond

- **James Bond:** wants to save the world
- **Villain:** wants to destroy the world

Batman

- **Batman:** wants to maintain order
- **Joker:** wants to bring chaos
- **Riddler:** wants confusion

Jojo Rabbit

- **Johannes 'Jojo' Betzler:** wants to be a good Nazi
- **Hitler:** wants Jojo to be a Nazi

Joker

- **Joker:** wants to be seen as funny (i.e., humorous)
- **Society:** thinks he's funny (i.e., weird)

Don't Look Up

- **Astronomers:** want people to take an oncoming comet seriously
- **Everyone else:** huh?

The Father

- **Anthony:** wants certainty
- **His mind:** generates confusion

Another Round

- **Teachers:** want excitement
- **Alcohol:** wants addicts

I've tried to show that it's not as simple as the protagonist wants one thing and the antagonist wants the opposite. Sometimes they want the **same thing**. Here's two examples in more depth:

Severance

In *Severance*, each of the main characters lives in two states: their day form who goes to work (Innie) and their non-work persona (Outie) who exists outside the office building.

- **Mark (Innie):** model employee
- **Mark (Outie):** nothing's going right
- **Irving (Innie):** a stickler for the rules
- **Irving (Outie):** cataloguing other severed people
- **Dylan (Innie):** fatherly
- **Dylan (Outie):** laddish
- **Helena (Innie):** hates being severed
- **Helena (Outie):** advocate for severance

The beauty of *Severance*'s premise is that each character is their **own** worst enemy. As the veil between their two sides is lifted, it leads to conflict.

Three Billboards Outside Ebbing, Missouri

- **Mildred:** wants justice
- **Police:** want justice

Here, both sides want the **same** thing. However, conflict still occurs because Mildred treats the police as the antagonist, rather than her daughter's killer (who's unknown). Her anger, at least on the surface, is fuelled by their failure to find him.

The police also want to catch the killer and are equally frustrated. Neither Mildred or the police can get what they want, despite doing everything they can to try to get it.

Does that mean you don't get a resolution in Act 3? In fact, we do. In the final scene, Mildred and a police officer form a partnership to track down a rapist. He's not the killer of Mildred's daughter, but he has escaped (formal) justice. By working together, they merge their thematic positions.

APHORISMS

Aphorisms are a valuable tool to express your idea or theme, in a familiar sentence or phrase. An aphorism is a short observation about life that rings true. Bear in mind for every aphorism, there's usually a contradicting one. Some examples:

- If you lie down with dogs, you wake up with fleas
- You can kill a man, but you can't kill an idea
- You can't trick a trickster
- It takes a thief to catch a thief

These aphorisms could be applied to several movies. The first could be any that involved an ingénue (an innocent) that joins a dangerous organisation, such as a cartel or criminal organisation e.g. *Goodfellas*. The last one could describe the premise of *Blade Runner*. If you need to find some aphorisms, there are plenty of lists available online.

IDIOMS

An idiom is a group of words that describe a feeling or a state of mind. Like aphorisms, they can sound corny or clichéd. But they provide a way to neatly sum up a situation, using a phrase most people will understand. This can be useful when pitching an idea. Some examples:

- Left high and dry
- Spill the beans
- To get on one's nerves

Be aware that many don't cross cultures or work in other languages. For example, the Swedish idiom, 'att glida in på en räkmacka', describes somebody hired through luck or nepotism. But it's literal translation is, 'to slide in on a shrimp sandwich'.

03.

STRUCTURE

A solid structure is your best bet of writing something that feels like a story. It's also the thing that no one watching or reading cares about, especially if you entertain them. The reason to understand structure, is it helps in writing an engaging story.

At this point, if you've completed some of the earlier sections, you might have some beat cards, an outline, or a bunch of scenes, perhaps written as sequences.

At last, you can finally start writing the script, can't you? Well, you could – there are no rules, remember. You might need to brush up on formatting first. There are books on it or just download a screenplay and study its form. This doesn't mean your action lines will be poetic straight away, but they'll look right. Screenwriting software can also help. There are plenty of options, many with free versions, such as *Final Draft*, *Arc Studio*, *Highland*, and *Causality*. In the last chapter, I'll give some tips too.

Where do you start, as you put pen to paper or fingers to keyboard? I'd suggest starting at page 1, but it doesn't matter. Start wherever you want: at the end, or in the middle of a scene that burns bright in your imagination. Write in sequence or out of sequence. Your decision may depend on the work you've done so far. But what if you're not quite ready to start your script? If that's the case, you've come to the right place!

SHAPE

This section concerns the shape of your story. Its size, where it begins and ends, and how many ups and downs our protagonist experiences. Shape can vary widely, but some have stood the test of time. Kurt Vonnegut's 4-minute lecture on the *Shapes of Stories* describes many of them. Most stories resemble a mountain and the experience of early skiers. They trudged to the top in snowshoes with wooden skis strapped to their backs. At the top, they pause to take in the view (the physical midpoint), then swoosh back down on skis.

ACTS

Stories usually have three Acts: a beginning (Act 1), a middle (Act 2), and an end (Act 3). An Act is a familiar phrase in theatre, that doesn't neatly translate to screenplays. A stage play is usually one Act or two. If it's two, the second Act occurs after the intermission. A single Act play, such as those at fringe festivals, runs for about an hour non-stop. A play you'd see at a posh theatre usually has a one-hour first Act, an intermission, and a shorter second Act. Unless it's by Jez Butterworth, where you might have two intervals in a three-hour play. These Acts describe more the format of the evening than they do the story's structure. Plays will still have three Acts – in terms of a beginning, middle, and end, with the intermission at the end of Act 2.

When talking about screenplays, an Act means something different, and is less visible to the viewer. An Act is a chunk of a story, each with its own beginning, middle, and end. Each Act ends with a significant event ('!' in the image below). At the start of each Act, there's often a different location, a time jump, or newly acquired knowledge.

Act 1 → ! Act 2 → ! Act 3 → !

Most feature screenplays are at least three Acts, whereas a short film is often one or two. Films that have more than three Acts, have an Act 1 and 2, and several second Acts. Some longer-form stories are less than three Acts e.g. *Waiting for Godot*, is just the second Act. Vladimir and Estragon are told to wait by the unseen, ominous Godot, and the play finishes before he arrives. We can argue that it isn't a story, as it has no Act 1 or 3, but it's entertaining, which is what matters most.

One can compare *Waiting for Godot*'s premise to the Chinese restaurant episode from *Seinfeld*. The three main characters are also stuck in limbo, waiting for a table. They're in a rush as they're trying to catch a movie. This episode was filmed live which was highly unusual at the time. The proposal was initially rejected by the network, as they didn't think it would work, because it had no story. Today, it's revered and inspired others to shoot live or make *bottle episodes* (more on these later).

A story that doesn't use all three Acts has specific consequences. In *Waiting for Godot*, you don't know much about the character's backstory, and you never find out if Godot turns up. If your script finishes at the end of Act 1, it's a **mystery**. If it ends after the second Act, it's a **tragedy**. In *Waiting for Godot*, there's a possibility that Vladimir and Estragon might be waiting forever.

At the end of the first Act, your protagonist goes from somewhere familiar to somewhere new (just as Vladimir and Estragon do when they arrive on stage). If you don't see the new environment, you're left to wonder what it's like and what might happen next (hence a mystery). Consider a *Doctor Who* story where you follow someone who enters the Tardis for the first time. They've gone from their home, usually Earth, into something magical. You don't get to see what happens to them if the episode stops when they go inside. Which could be a good way to end an episode. Only if the story moves onto Act 2, do we find out where our protagonist (and new assistant) go.

A story that runs for just the first two Acts finishes in tragic circumstances. The end of Act 2 is a low point for our protagonist. When they reach it, they'll feel like everything's gone wrong. That all their effort so far has been pointless. Things usually turnaround in Act 3. Most stories finish with a mostly upbeat ending. Act 3 gives us time to get to our happyish ending. Not all stories do this. *Macbeth*, *Breaking Bad*, or *Boiling Point* finish with our protagonist's death. They are still 3-Act stories, but end in tragedy.

When a story has more than three Acts, it's still a story told in three parts, but with several Act 2s. Shakespeare famously used five Acts although this could be due to publishing practices, how long candles lasted, or toilet breaks. A modern example of a story with more than three Acts is *Raiders of the Lost Ark* which has five Acts. Here they are:

- **Act 1:** in Peru, Indiana Jones recovers an idol, but has it taken from him. He's told about a Nazi plan to find the Ark of the Covenant
- **Act 2 (or 2a):** in Nepal, Indiana recovers a medallion linked to the Ark
- **Act 3 (or 2b):** in Cairo, Indy uses the medallion to determine the Ark's resting place. He retrieves it, but is captured by the Nazis
- **Act 4 (or 2c):** Indy escapes with the Ark to London by sea but is caught by the Nazis en route
- **Act 5 (or 3):** on an island, the Ark is opened, killing the Nazis. The Ark is recovered and hidden

Acts 2, 3, and 4, are part of an expanded, or repeated, Act 2. Each occurs in different locations. Acts 3 and 4 end with a turning point that temporarily halts Indy's attempts to recover the Ark. Splitting Act 2 into three parts (a, b, and c) provides clarity, prior to a conventional Act 3. This multi-Act structure is common in big-budget action films like *James Bond* or *Mission Impossible*. Each second has its own beginning, middle, and end, usually set in a fresh location. Each Act fills out the story from the middle, like an ever expanding Christmas cracker, but maintaining its familiar symmetrical shape.

SYMMETRY

Symmetry is appealing. We see it in nature in the shape of a leaf or a tree. Draw a line down the middle and both sides will look similar. Symmetry is characterised by significant structural elements being repeated, often mirrored. Models and actors usually have symmetrical faces, that might subtly signal good health. I believe a favourable bias exists with stories too. I don't think every element needs its opposing partner. But having some is helpful. The key to using symmetry is make sure the pairs are similar but different. And often opposite.

To understand how we can use symmetry, start with a piece of paper – A4 in portrait mode will do. Next, draw a line horizontally across the middle (Figure 9).

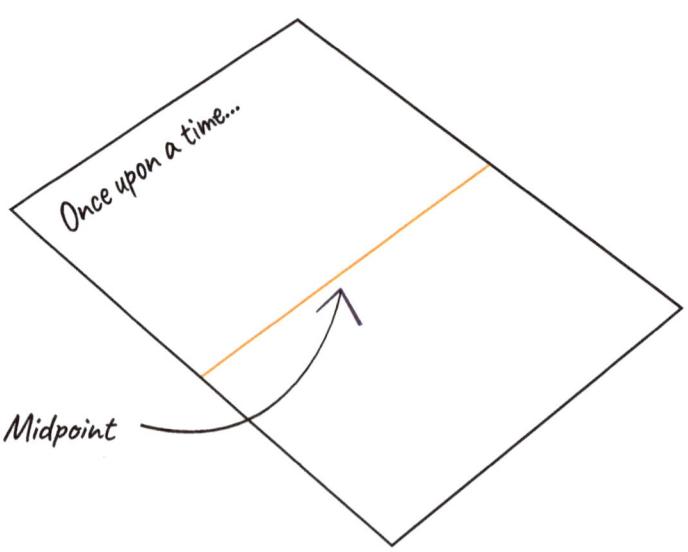

Figure 9: Symmetry Exercise Step 1.

The top side is the first half of your story, and the bottom is the second half, with Act 2 split across the Midpoint (Figure 10).

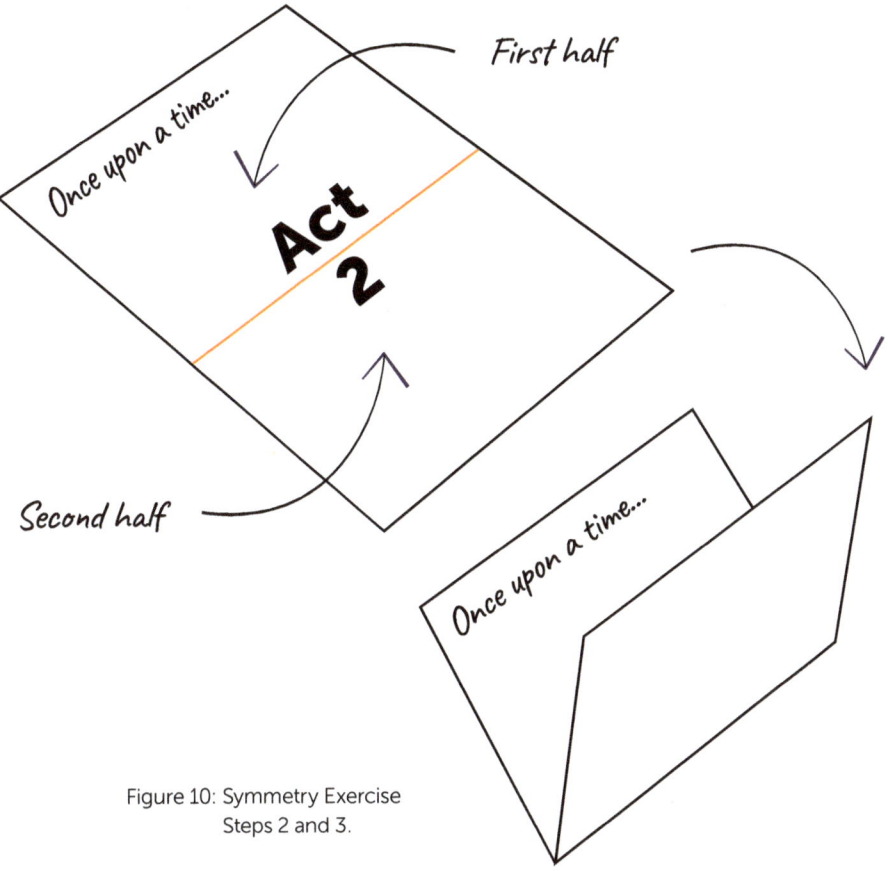

Figure 10: Symmetry Exercise Steps 2 and 3.

Now, instead of prose, let's imagine you've written it as single-sentence scene summaries. Perhaps a dozen above the line and the same below. If you fold the page along the line, the two halves would be on top of each other. The last scene is squashed against the first scene. The penultimate scene against the second scene. And so on. Each scene has its sibling. But are they twins? And how do you make practical use of this? Let's return to Schrader's scene sheet, with Act 1 and Act 2 approximations, and the Pages columns removed (Table 3).

#	SCENE	#	SCENE
1		29	
2		30	
3		31	
4		32	
5		33	
6		34	
7		35	
8		36	
9		37	
10		38	
11		39	
12		40	
13		41	
14	End of Act 1	42	
15		43	
16		44	
17		45	
18		46	End of Act 2
19		47	
20		48	
21		49	
22		50	
23		51	
24		52	
25		53	
26		54	
27		55	
28		56	

Table 3: Scene Sheet.

In the Scene Sheet, scenes run from the top of the left column down, then start again at the top of the second column. The Midpoint is somewhere around the bottom of the first column and the top of the second column (27-30). It's a useful table but doesn't help much in looking for symmetry. Now look at Table 4, my Symmetry Table.

#	SCENE	#	SCENE
25		26	
24		27	
23		28	
22	*Midpoint*	29	*Midpoint*
21		30	
20		31	
19		32	
18		33	
17		34	
16		35	
15		36	
14		37	
13		38	
12		39	
11		40	
10		41	
9		42	
8	*End of Act 1*	43	
7		44	
6		45	
5		46	*End of Act 2*
4		47	
3		48	
2		49	
1		50	

Table 4: Symmetry Table.

Here, you can see that I've reversed the scene positions in the first column so scene 1 is now at the bottom. I've created it with 50 scenes but you could have any number. Column 2 stays the same. Firstly, this means that all the scenes that could be at the Midpoint are now at the top of the page. Secondly, the first scene is now opposite the last scene, and the second is next to the penultimate one. And so on. It's now structured like our folded piece of paper, but everything is still visible. And finally, when viewing it from the

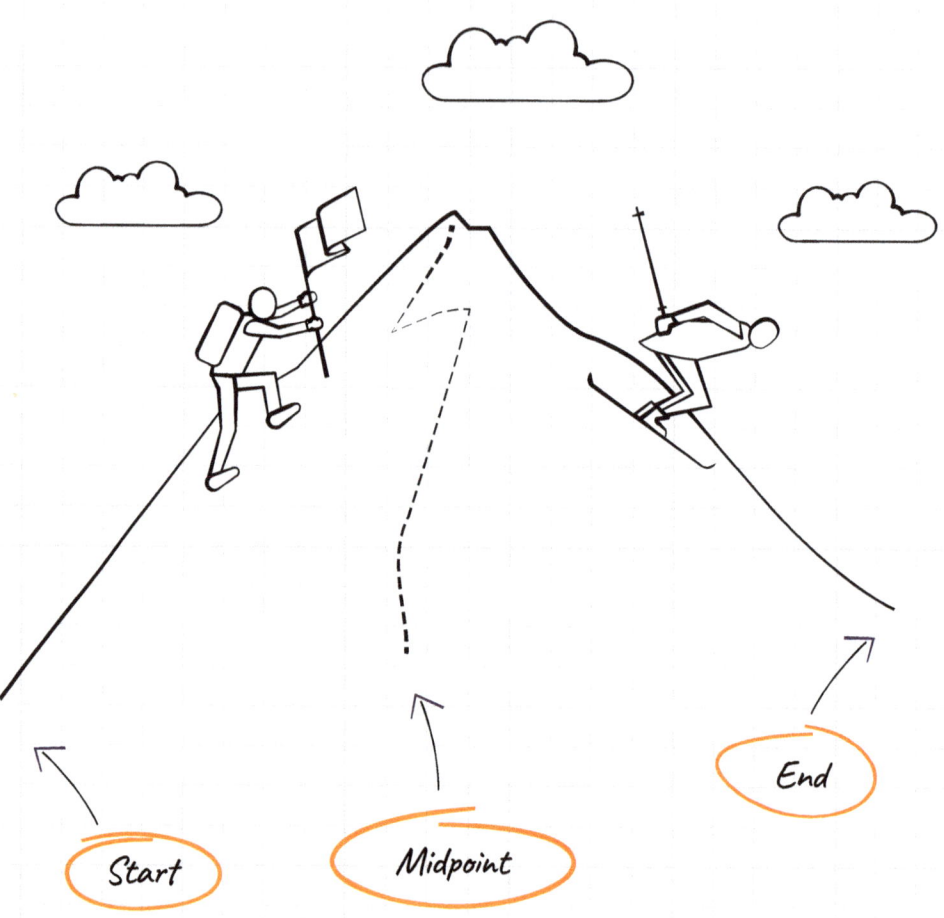

Figure 11: Up and Down the Mountain.

first scene, up to the top and back down again, it feels like you're on a journey. With the paper laid flat, you move away from your body, get to the Midpoint, turn 180 degrees around, to head back towards yourself. It's like an inverted U or a mountain (Figure 11).

Robocop is an example of a film with plenty of symmetry. In fact, almost every scene has a mirrored opposite and was first described by Robert Lockard (the Deja Reviewer). He called it a **scenic palindrome**. It's an example of a chiasmus, which occur frequently in the Bible's Old Testament. For example, Jesus Christ said to his disciples, 'Many that are first shall be last, and the last shall be first.' This sentence is a chiasmus – the words in the second half are a mirror image of those in the first half. He used it to explain that it didn't matter when you took the right path in life because you'd all arrive at the same place (i.e. heaven).

Now we have this tool, how can you use it? One way is to analyse a film. I've added Page columns, which refer to the page in the script that the scene occurs, removed the Act Break lines, and increased the number of rows to accommodate my example, *Sound of Metal* (Table 5). I've also included beats as well as scenes.

#	SCENE OR BEAT	PAGE	#	SCENE OR BEAT	PAGE
38	Ruben writes in the study.	55	39	Ruben sits in the study.	57
37	Ruben signs with the kids.	55	40	Ruben's buddy leaves	57-8
36	Ruben drums for one of the kids.	55	41	Ruben asked to stay if he wants.	59
35	Ruben watches show.	54	42	Ruben watches Lou perform solo.	60
34	Ruben stands in study room.	54	43	Ruben sells some of his gear.	61
33	Ruben refuses to drum for the kids.	53-4	44	Ruben and the kids drum together.	62
32	Joe tells him to focus on himself.	49-53	45	Ruben looks after Michael	63
31	Ruben fixes broken shutter.	49	46	Ruben and Diane chat alone.	63
30	Ruben talks about his addiction.	48	47	Ruben finds Jenn has not returned.	63
29	Kids pray about acceptance.	48	48	Ruben tries to go into town.	64
28	Joe reads a supportive email from Lou.	47-8	49	Jenn has overdosed using Ruben's cash.	64
27	Joe learns ASL and they learn graffiti.	44-7	50	Ruben finds his Airstream keys.	65
26	Joe joins a children's deaf class.	44-7	51	Ruben phones Prince Audiology.	65
25	Joe meets others. Gets objectives.	42-3	52	Ruben sells Airstream.	67
24	Ruben gets room, gives up phone, keys.	42	53	Ruben leaves.	68
23	Lou makes Ruben promise to go back.	39-41	54	Ruben has implants fitted.	68
22	Lou phones someone. Lou and Ruben argue.	36-8	55	Ruben shows Joe the implants.	69
21	Ruben removes music equipment.	36	56	Joe suggests that inner peace comes from stillness.	71
20	Joe tells Lou to find a safe place to go.	34-5	57	Ruben asks Joe for money.	72
19	Joe tells them Ruben must be alone.	32-33	58	Joe asks Ruben to leave.	73-4
18	Joe explains they fix heads not ears.	30-1	59	Ruben leaves. Goes to hospital.	74
17	Discuss Lou, music, implants.	29-30	60	Ruben's implants are activated.	75
16	Discuss deafness and addictions.	26-9	61	Ruben goes to Paris.	76
15	A transcription device is set up.	24-6	62	Ruben enters Lou's father's posh flat.	77
14	Meets the owner, Joe.	22-4	63	Richard is preparing for a party.	77
13	Travel to deaf community.	20-2	64	Richard talks about being true to one's nature.	78
12	Ruben talks to psychologist.	18-9	65	Ruben talks childhood, travelling.	79
11	Ruben smokes. Lou's angry.	17	66	Richard reveals that his ex-wife took Louise.	80
10	Ruben and Lou discuss it.	16	67	Richard thanks Ruben for looking after Lou.	81
9	Ruben starts the gig but runs out.	15	68	Lou returns, looking healthy.	81
8	Ruben is told to stop playing.	8-15	69	The party starts. Ruben is out of place.	84
7	Ruben is deaf. Seeks help.	7	70	Richard and Lou sing together.	85
6	Ruben experiences tinnitus.	6	71	Ruben and Lou talk.	85-9
5	Ruben and Lou chat in RV.	4-6	72	Ruben realises that going on tour would make Lou sick.	89
4	Ruben and Lou dance.	3	73	Ruben and Lou agree they saved each other.	89
3	Ruben makes breakfast.	2-3	74	Ruben steps outside into the noise.	90
2	Ruben and Lou. It's sleepy, quiet.	1	75	Ruben wide awake. It's loud.	90
1	Ruben and Lou play metal in a club.	1	76	Ruben sits alone in silence. At peace.	90

Table 5: Symmetry Table (Sound of Metal).

Sound of Metal

In this film, a hyperactive, hard rock drummer, Ruben, loses his hearing and tries to figure out how to play again, while searching for inner peace. Table 6 shows *Sound of Metal* as a Symmetry Table. It doesn't include every scene, just the scenes where something significant occurs. I've indicated the end of Acts 1 and 2. At the end of Act 1, Ruben goes to Joe's deaf community and at the end of Act, 2, he goes to Paris. Act 1 occupies ~22 % of the script, Act 2, ~51 %, and Act 3, ~16 %, in terms of pages. This is a typical distribution for a feature film.

I've also highlighted the Midpoint: scenes 38 and 39, where Ruben demonstrates a significant change in his behaviour. In scene 38, Ruben writes furiously in the study, but in scene 39, he sits still. A 180-degree pivot – characteristic of a Midpoint. His counsellor told Ruben early in the film that he'd achieve serenity if he made peace with the past. Through free writing, he achieves that, and gazes outside.

Interestingly, my Midpoint is not in the middle of the 90-page script, but occurs on pages 55-57. The mathematical Midpoint should be around page 45. At this point of the story, Ruben joins the kid's classroom for the first time. He goes from being the person generally in charge – as we've seen from his relationship with Lou (as well as something he'd been forced to do as a child), to being treated like a child again. Both seem valid as Midpoints. I'll discuss Midpoints more later.

In Table 5, I've highlighted pairs of scenes from *Sound of Metal* that are opposites. They are:

- 1 and 76
- 3 and 64
- 4 and 74
- 7 and 70
- 9 and 69
- 12 and 64
- 13 and 62
- 18 and 59
- 22 and 51
- 23 and 54
- 24 and 50
- 30 and 47
- 33 and 44
- 35 and 42

That's 14 pairs that mostly sit directly opposite their partner. Let's go through them.

SCENES 1 AND 76
At the film's start, Ruben and Lou play heavy rock in a sweaty, dark bar. In scene 76, he sits alone in total silence, his hearing implants removed. There's a stark contrast between these two images. In the first, he's full of energy – arms flailing and noise flooding his senses. In the last moment of the film , he's at peace, sitting still.

SCENES 3 AND 64
In scene 3, Ruben makes breakfast for Lou as she dozes in bed. He's full of energy and blitzes a smoothie. Whether she wants it or not is unclear. In scene 64, her father, Richard, encourages Ruben to have some of the breakfast he's making. Richard beats the eggs furiously as Ruben sits uncomfortably

SCENES 4 AND 74
As part of their morning ritual, Ruben and Lou dance outside the RV before setting off (scene 4). In scene 74, they hug in Lou's bedroom, Ruben leaves alone.

SCENES 7 AND 70
In scene 7, Ruben, now deaf, is told to stop playing. In scene 70, Richard and Lou sing together as Ruben watches.

SCENES 9 AND 69
In scene 9, Ruben is at home, comfortable behind a drum kit. In scene 69, Ruben is out of place, at a posh dinner party.

SCENES 12 AND 64
In scene 12, Ruben speaks to his psychologist and is reminded that serenity comes from accepting the past. In scene 64, Richard tells him that a leopard can't change its spots.

SCENES 13 AND 62
In scene 13, Rube arrives at Joe's rural community for deaf children and adults with addictions. In scene 62, Ruben arrives at Richard's swanky Paris flat.

SCENES 18 AND 59
In scene 18, Joe explains to Ruben that he fixes heads not hearing. In scene 59, Ruben leaves the retreat to restore his hearing with his mind unhealed.

SCENES 22 AND 51
In scene 22, Lou phones Richard for help. In scene 51, Ruben speaks to Prince Audiology to confirm his appointment.

SCENES 23 AND 54
In scene 23, Lou makes Ruben promise to return to Joe's (to fix his head and learn American Sign Language). In scene 54, Ruben has his implants fitted.

SCENES 24 AND 50
In scene 24, Ruben gives the keys to his Airstream to Joe. In scene 50, Ruben steals the keys back.

SCENES 30 AND 47
In scene 30, Ruben talks to Joe about his addiction to drugs. In scene 47, Ruben's buddy, Jenn, has overdosed.

SCENES 33 AND 44
In scene 33, Ruben refuses to drum for the kids. In scene 44, Ruben and the kids drum together.

SCENES 35 AND 42
In scene 35, Ruben watches the show put on for the kids. In scene 42, Ruben watches as Lou performs without him.

All the pairs straddle the Midpoint and include Ruben. What do these chiasmas achieve? They demonstrate how different Ruben is in the second half of the story compared to the first. They show how he has changed – a fundamental element of stories. And what better way to show this than to present pairs of contrasting but similar scenes.

Cell Mates

The example above was quite technical and involved, but it doesn't have to be. The stage play, *Cell Mates*, by Simon Gray dramatises George Blake's escape from Wormwood Scrubs and his time in Russia. Blake had been convicted of spying for the Russians and sentenced to 42 years. An Irishman, Sean Bourke, helped him escape to Moscow but Blake prevents him from returning home. I'll designate George the protagonist and Sean the antagonist, but it could work the other way around. They both want the same thing – to publish an account of their daring deed – and believe that only one book should be published. (George's book will justify his reasons for spying, while Sean's will describe his ingenuity). Cell Mates is a full-length play, so has two Acts, either side of an interval. In Table 6, you can see them side-by-side and how they mirror each other. In the first Act, George is trapped, and Sean has the power to release him. In the second Act, the dynamic is reversed: Sean is trapped in Russia, and George can have him released (or not).

ACT 1	ACT 2
George is a guest in Sean's office.	Sean is a guest in George's office/home.
George needs Sean to help him escape.	Sean is trapped by George.
George is watched closely.	Sean is watched closely.
George has hope (to leave) then regret.	Sean has regret (for coming) but hope.
Sean knows where the power lies (Prison System).	George knows where the power lies (KGB).
George is dishevelled.	Sean is dishevelled.
George is disorientated.	Sean is drunk.
Sean looks after George.	George looks after Sean.

Table 6: Cell Mates Symmetry Table.

Passengers

In this film about a ship full of sleeping colonists, Jim Preston is woken prematurely by a fault with his stasis pod. Jim's alone and will die before they reach their destination. He wakes a female sleeper, Aurora, telling her that her pod was faulty. They grow close until she learns the truth. She shuns him. After a few twists and turns, where he demonstrates heroism, she forgives him, and they spend 'eternity' together. An alternative ending, driven by symmetry, would be for Jim to help Aurora into the last remaining working pod and become the ship's human custodian: the ultimate hero.

Using symmetry as a tool has several specific uses:

1. To analyse a story's structure for existing symmetry
2. To align symmetrical scenes
3. To create new scenes using symmetry

The **Symmetry Table** also allows you to mark your Act breaks, the Midpoint, and the page splits between Acts. I think it's a powerful tool.

CIRCLES

A popular method to visualise a story's structure is based on circles. The protagonist starts at the top and travels clockwise around the circumference and finishes where they started. It can help to the visualise the circle as a clock with each hour a stage of their journey, or the playing piece from Trivial Pursuit with its slices of pie. Using the clock metaphor, we can see there's symmetry: 12 is opposite 6, 1 opposite 7, 2 opposite 8, and so on.

We could also split the circle into Acts:

- **Act 1:** 20%
- **Act 2:** 65%
- **Act 3:** 15%

For a standard 90-page script, those percentages translate to, 13, 68, and nine pages. As a clock it's roughly: Act 1: 12-3, Act 2: 3-9, and Act 3: 9-12 (Figure 12).

Circles can be used in a different way. Imagine a stone thrown into a pond. Circular ripples radiate out from the impact. Each ring is larger than the one inside it. Moving from the smallest circle to the largest is like a story expanding through its telling. Every circle relates to its origin despite moving further away. If we imagine the centre as the **theme**, each new circle carries a memory of it as it expands and dissipates. Your theme should be present in every beat, scene, or Act (Figure 13).

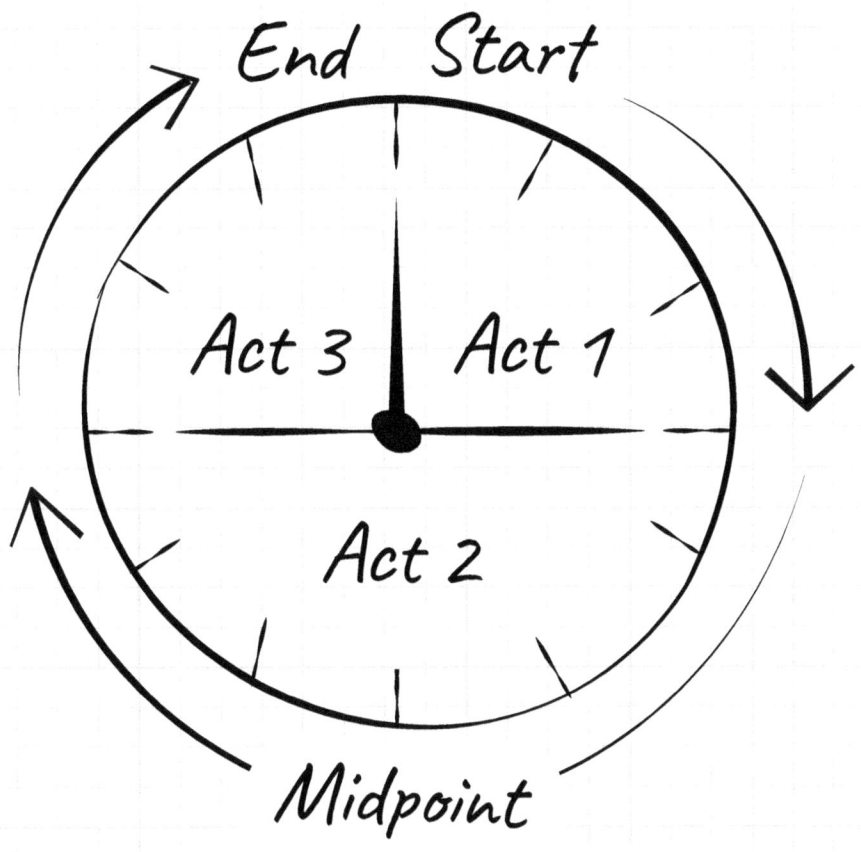

Figure 12: The 3-Act Structure as a Clock.

For a long-running series, you can expand it further (Figure 13). In long-running series like *Breaking Bad*, *Succession*, or *Game of Thrones*, the writers have the time to examine theme in depth. In *Breaking Bad*, the theme could be 'power corrupts; absolute power corrupts absolutely'. Walt starts as a decent man with good intentions, but as he gains power (through his expertise, growing influence, and by making money), his moral compass goes increasingly awry. Having a strong central theme anchors a story as it expands.

An alternative to using theme as a glue is to replace it with an institutional, geographical, or cultural perspective. For example, in *The Wire*, the characters remained mostly the same, each progressing in their lives, but the overarching perspective on them changed e.g. the docks, children, or the newspapers. In this case, our circle becomes a sphere, with the POV changing as we move around it.

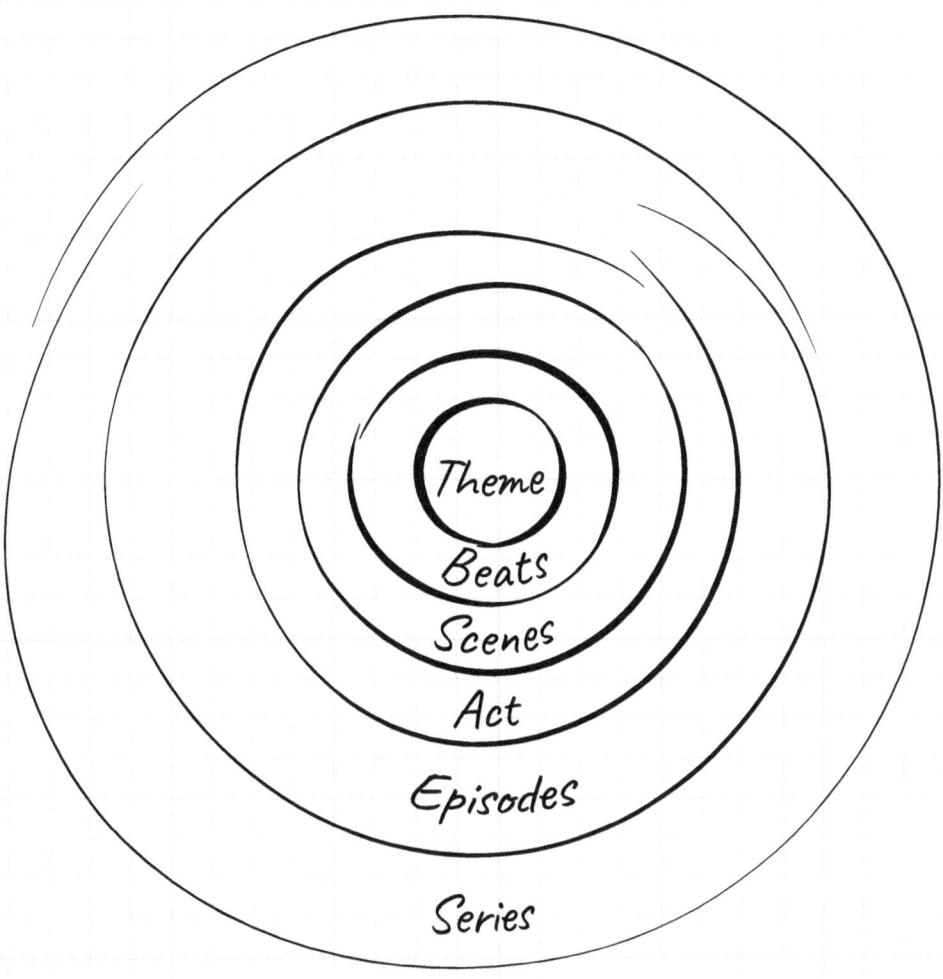

Figure 13: Theme Radiating Out Like Ripples on Water.

MUSIC

Music shares some structural similarities with stories, such as symmetry and theme. Many ancient stories were traditionally sung e.g. folk music and sea shanties. Popular music also has a common structure: verse, chorus, verse, chorus, middle eight, and chorus. Songs tend to be in a key with a defined tempo, similar to a theme and genre. They tend to begin slowly, reach a midpoint, where there's a change (the middle eight), before continuing to the end, repeating earlier sections. And like a story Midpoint, the middle eight (or bridge) is a section where things change significantly.

Let's look at the song *Dakota* by Stereophonics, and examine its structure, first using verse, chorus and middle eight:

Figure 14: Song Structure of Dakota by Stereophonics.

And now with their lengths (minutes and seconds):

- **0-50:** Verse
- **50-1:05:** First chorus
- **1:05-1:30:** Verse
- **1:30-1:55:** Second chorus (twice)
- **2:00-2:25:** Middle eight
- **2:25-2:50:** Verse
- **2:50-3:15:** Third chorus (twice)
- **3:15-4:00:** Middle eight (twice)

What if we split the song down the middle:

First Half		**Second Half**
• Verse		• Verse
• Chorus	Middle eight	• Chorus
• Verse		• Chorus
• Chorus		• Middle eight
• Chorus	•	• Middle eight

There is some mirror symmetry just as we saw with *Sound of Metal*. Only once does two of the same elements sit opposite each other. Like the **Symmetry Table**, the same but different.

STORYSAURUS
(BY AMY ROSENTHAL)

A story is a path of rising action. And the action should be dramatic with unexpected outcomes. In Figure 15, I've drawn a path that meanders along, always rising. At some points it gets tougher, and our protagonist has to climb a slope. Finally, they face a steep climb to the top, where the journey ends.

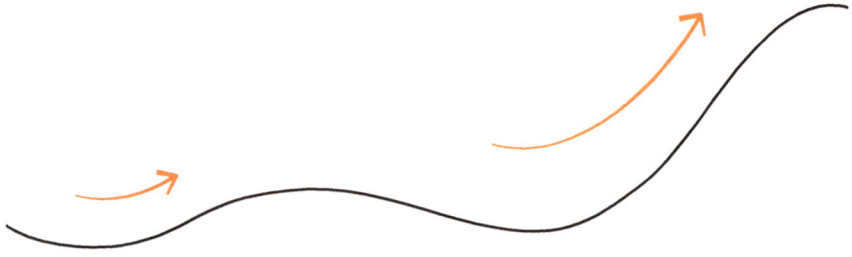

Figure 15: The Path of Dramatic Action.

This is rather bland story, so let's fill our Hero's Journey with peril, emotions, characters, challenges, and surprise. Doing so, the picture starts to take shape (Figure 16).

Figure 16: Filling Out Your Story.

Our story's nearly complete. It just needs a bit of finessing. Perhaps a thematic question has emerged during the writing process. Or you a come up with a great Midpoint or how the protagonist's defeats the antagonist. With these additions, your **storysaurus** is alive.

Figure 17: A Storysaurus.

OPENING AND CLOSING IMAGES

The opening and closing images are the visual bookends of a story. As a pair, they summarise the protagonists' journey. The first images have an additional role as they set the tone, usually introduce the protagonist, and give a sense of what the story's about. In *Star Wars: Episode IV: A New Hope*, Darth Vader's Executor ship rumbles over our heads, pursuing a small spaceship trying to escape. It tells us this story is about the big guy bullying the little guy (thought to be a reference to the Vietnam War). Christopher Nolan quipped that the opening image in *Memento* – a polaroid undeveloping, 'was pretty much the whole movie.'

The opening images of our protagonist can also clue us in to their state of mind, their flaw, and even what's to come. In *Sound of Metal*, Ruben's doing what he loves – playing the drums. But there's something not quite right about it, which is hinted at in the action line of the script, 'Sweat drips from Ruben's hair and his eyes burn in an endless climax... or (sic) pain.' In the opening scenes of *Toy Story*, Woody is hyperactive in his attempts to corral the other toys. In *One Flew Over The Cuckoo's Nest*, Murphy is sent to a mental asylum and tells the Governor, 'Now they're telling me I'm crazy over here cuz I don't sit here like a goddamn *vegetable*.'

Opening images can do a lot. They can show us our protagonist, their passion, and their environment and hint at something troubling them. By indicating that everything's not all right in their current existence, you set up the possibility of them changing it. The closing images present the conclusion of a story. In most cases, it features our protagonist, even if on the point of death e.g. *Rogue One: A Star Wars Story*. You may not remember the opening shots, but you'll know that things have changed.

An exception is traditional sitcoms, where a reset occurs after each episode, that returns everything to where it was at the start. These sitcoms were common in the days of scheduled programming with a week between episodes. By having each episode start from the same point, audiences didn't have to remember what had happened previously. This format now feels outdated. And even successful franchises such as James Bond, have felt the pressure to demonstrate some emotional growth of their protagonist, even if others e.g. John Wick, seem to benefit from an absence of personality. Let's look at some examples of opening and closing images:

Sound of Metal

- **Opening Images:** Ruben plays drums in a club
- **Closing Images:** Ruben sits in silence on a park bench

The Queen's Gambit

- **Opening Images:** Beth, hungover and asleep in her hotel room's empty bath, is woken by a knock on the door
- **Closing Images:** Beth, dressed immaculately in white, strolls along a busy street

Memories of Murder

- **Opening Images:** two women are found raped and murdered. The incompetent local detective, Park Doo-Man, believes he can find the killer simply by using eye contact
- **Closing Images:** another woman is killed, and no one's caught. Park Doo-Man, no longer a detective, visits the crime scene years later, still reliant on his eye contact method

Squid Game

- **Opening Images:** Seong Gi-hun is poor, wears a t-shirt and shorts, and lives with his mother, earning a small income as a chauffeur. He gambles on horses
- **Closing Images:** Seong Gi-hun is rich, in a suit with dyed hair. He's leaving the country but stops. He tells the game's organisers he's not a horse and turns back

Memento

- **Opening Images:** Leonard Shelby kills a man and takes a Polaroid picture of the body
- **Closing Images:** Leonard Shelby kills a man and takes a Polaroid picture of the body

Nightmare Alley

- **Opening Images:** Stanton Carlisle, clean and dressed, wraps a body, buries it under the floorboards of a house, which he sets fire to
- **Closing Images:** Stanton Carlisle, messy and dirty, agrees to become a caged exhibit in a circus

Rogue One: A Star Wars Story

- **Opening Images:** an Imperial officer kidnaps an engineer to help them build the Death Star
- **Closing Images:** the engineer's daughter sends the Death Star's schematics to Princess Leia

The opening and closing images in *Sound of Metal*, *The Queen's Gambit*, and *Squid Game* are opposites. In each, the protagonist has transformed, both internally (chaos to peace, addicted to clean, selfish to selfless) and externally (no hearing aids to hearing implants, anonymous to famous, poor to rich). All are examples of significant changes to the protagonist. In all three, the protagonist has undergone a significant transformation, a common structural choice in most stories, achieved through dynamic plotting, with cause and effect.

In *Memories of Murder*, Park Doo-Man is no longer a detective, perhaps through incompetence or a change of heart. But he still clings to the belief in his supernatural ability (which may have ended his career). In *Nightmare Alley*, Stanton Carlisle looks very different at the end compared to the start of the film. But in essence, he's the same person: a nasty, cruel individual, who deserves to be locked up in a cage. Leonard Shelby, who can't form new memories, relentlessly searches for his wife's killer. When he thinks he's found them, he kills them, forgets what he's done and begins the cycle again. None of these protagonists have changed, but their world has. In *Memories of Murder*, another woman has died; in *Nightmare Alley*, the circus has a new freak, and in *Memento*, an innocent man is dead.

In my final example, *Rogue One*, a group of Rebel Alliance soldiers try to steal the plans for the Death Star, a new and powerful Imperial weapon. They succeed in their mission, but die doing so. This outcome – not a typical 'Hollywood' one – is fitting for the genre. This wasn't a fantasy like previous *Star Wars* films but a war movie, more similar to *Band of Brothers* or *The Guns of Navarone*. The final images of the two remaining rebels, awaiting their death, has echoes of the first scenes, when Imperial storm troopers arrive to take Jyn for a life of servitude. But, like her mother, she chooses freedom, even if it means death.

04.

PLOT

In this third section, I'll talk plot — what happens. Plot usually refers only to the external elements of the story that affect your protagonist. However, I have two: a Mind Plot (external events) and a Heart Plot (internal changes). These two plots are intertwined like a rope. The Mind Plot is what the protagonist does (or has done to them) while the Heart Plot maps how events affect them emotionally. So we have:

1. **Mind Plot: what happens**

2. **Heart Plot: how they feel**

TWO PLOTS

Your Mind Plot should be clear, entertaining and led by an active protagonist. And if you need to prioritise one of those, make it enjoyable to watch or read. People will forgive a few plot holes if the story's fun. A Heart Plot gives you three dimensional characters who the audience can emphasise with. You can omit a Heart Plot but will have an emotionally hollow story. This might not be an issue if it's an action film, but even these benefit from a strong Heart Plot. Together, like two halves of a watermelon, both fill most of the space required for a Story Box (Figure 18).

The Mind Plot is made up of small action sequences when the protagonist does something or something is done to them. The results will be a mixture of successes, failures, surprises, and revelations. Each outcome determines the likelihood of them achieving their ultimate goal and how they feel (the Heart Plot). The protagonist, now feeling differently, may now change their behaviour. This is the cause-and-effect relationship between the Mind and Heart Plots.

The Mind and Heart plots have different elements. A Mind Plot can include:

- **Obstacles:** that the protagonist tries to overcome
- **Turning points:** usually occur at the end of an Act and drastically changes the protagonist's knowledge or behaviour
- **Milestones:** an objective achieved (or not)
- **Surprises:** a secret revealed or an unexpected event

A Heart Plot contains:

- **Beats:** an emotional response to an event
- **Changes:** a new behaviour or outlook (emotional growth)

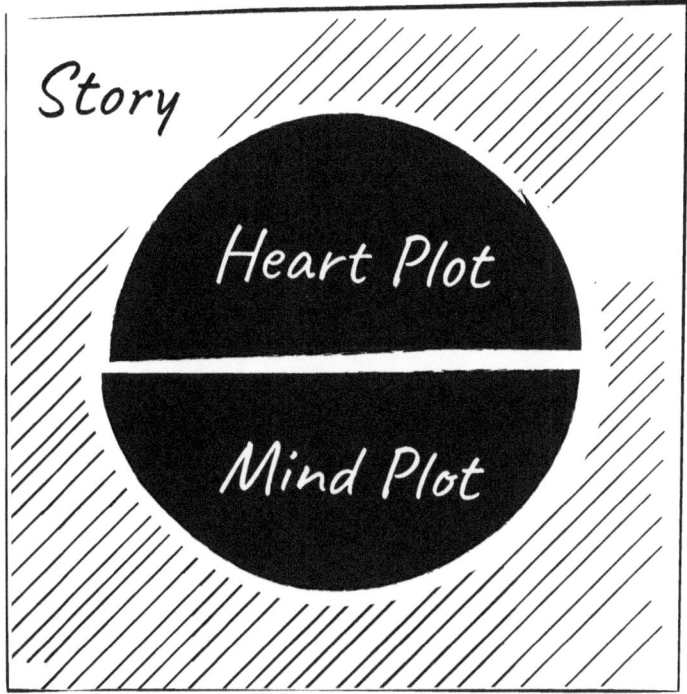

Figure 18: Story Box.

As has already been stated, it is possible to write a story with mostly Mind Plot. And if there's plenty of activity, it can still be engaging e.g. action films with stoic heroes. We get a visceral thrill from watching them cheat death, regardless of whether it bothers them. In fact, their inability to feel anything makes the relentless pursuit of their goal 'more' believable. But this type of protagonist isn't a fully formed character. And shouldn't that be worth trying to achieve? Take for example, *No Time to Die*, in which we had a James Bond who felt closer to a fully rounded human being than we've had before.

The Mind and Heart plots run side-by-side throughout the story. However, the Mind Plot starts and finishes first. After all, it's external events that affect how we feel. It may help to remember the idea of two plots by drawing attention to the phrase, 'winning hearts and minds', coined by Louis Hubert Gonzalve Lyautey in 1895. He was a French general and used the phrase to summarise his plan to counter the Black Flags rebellion along the Indochina-Chinese border. Although it's probably best known for being used by US President George W. Bush in relation to the invasion of Iraq.

By starting with the Mind Plot, you can grip the audience's attention quickly. By starting with an event (usually the Inciting Incident) that takes our protagonist by surprise, you create a situation that we want to see resolved. How will Woody, accustomed to being the top dog, cope with the arrival of a superior toy (*Toy Story*)? The Inciting Incident presents a challenge to our protagonist that they find hard to ignore. If you look close enough, the Heart Plot is set up first, but it's usually so subtle we don't notice.

Sometimes the Inciting Incident introduces a ticking clock – a time constraint for our protagonist to achieve a goal. It may be their ultimate goal e.g. to destroy an asteroid heading to earth or a bomb with a countdown timer. From the Inciting Incident onwards, the protagonist should be making choices on how to save the day e.g. whether to cut the red or blue wire. The outcomes of their choices will advance both plots.

The Heart Plot is the protagonist's internal reaction to the consequences of their actions (or the antagonist's). Like a melody, it should be 'long and flowing, with low and high points of interest and a climactic moment usually near the end' (Aaron Copeland, *What to Listen for in Music*). They're emotional state should fluctuate as a consequence of what happens (Figure 19).

The Heart Plot should also map how they overcome (or don't) a central flaw in their personality. This flaw is holding them back, preventing them from reaching their full potential or at its simplest, to be content or happy. The obstacles they encounter should test their flawed behaviour or mindset. They should fail. And with each failure, their resistance to addressing their flaw is eroded. Ultimately, they will make the decision whether to fix it or not, resulting in a significant outcome.

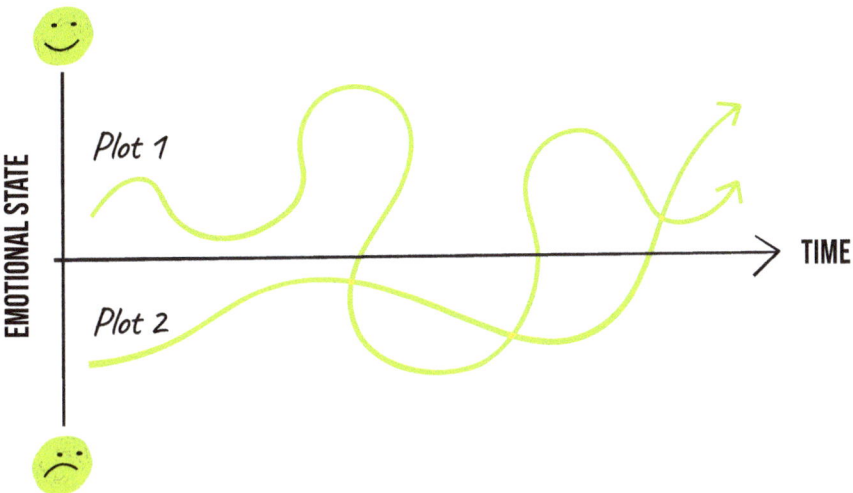

Figure 19: Heart Plot.

Bluebird

As an example of how the Heart and Mind Plots can be used, I'm going to use the play *Bluebird* by Simon Stephens. The play starts with the protagonist – a male taxi driver called Jimmy – calling someone to arrange a meeting to discuss something of importance. We don't hear the other person or the detail of what's discussed. This scene creates a mystery we're curious to see resolved (Mind Plot). At the end of the play we find out who he's meeting and why. In between, Jimmy picks up passengers and talks to them. These conversations have an emotional impact on him (Heart Plot).

The Mind Plot concludes when he meets his wife, Clare (the person on the phone), and it's revealed that he accidentally killed their daughter, then disappeared. Jimmy has spent the last five years working as a taxi driver and sleeping in the car. The Heart Plot's resolved when he apologises and offers Clare the money he's saved. They visit their daughter's grave together for the first time.

At the end of your story, the Heart and Mind Plots should be resolved. The Mind Plot resolves first through a final dramatic act by the protagonist. At the same time or shortly afterwards, the Heart Plot is resolved when they face their flaw. In *Of Mice and Men*, George's last act completes both plots simultaneously. He realises he can no longer protect Lennie from a cruel world (Lennie will be hung). So George decides to end Lennie's life to save him from the trauma of capture and incarceration. He accepts the burden of guilt to protect his best friend.

WANT

At the start of your story, your protagonist should have a clear (if misguided) picture of what their future will look like. And it needs to be conveyed to the audience. In *The Responder*, a counsellor asks Police Constable Chris Carson what he wants from the job: 'I just want to do good,' he replies. What the protagonist wants is often what they try to do on a day-to-day basis, like Chris. But they may also harbour some unfulfilled dream, like Lightning McQueen in *Cars*, who wants to win the Piston Cup. Or they might want society to change like Nelson Mandela (*Mandela*) or Dr. Martin Luther King Jr. (*Selma*).

In many stories, the protagonist wants to maintain the *status quo*. They appear on the surface to be satisfied with their life. But we can tell something's wrong even if they can't. When Chris elaborates on being a bobby, he reveals the futility of what he's doing: 'It's like Whac-A-Mole.' Further aggravation follows each success. This might be the norm but it's causing him pain. He makes a rash decision that sets off a cascade of events.

In other stories, the protagonist wants things to be different, or acquire knowledge, to solve a mystery, like Benoit Blanc.

To summarise, there are three types of want, each centred on the protagonist:

1. They want change
2. They don't want change (but need it)
3. They want knowledge

Let's go through each one with some examples.

WANT CHANGE

There are clear examples where the protagonist wants something to change. This might be something for themselves or for others. Richard Williams (*King Richard*) wants his daughters to succeed. *Forrest Gump* catalyses change in others. They all want their worlds to be different from how they are now. Luke Skywalker wants adventure. Dr. Martin Luther King Jr. wants equal voting rights (*Selma*). Others want a better life e.g. *The Pursuit of Happyness*. Others are following orders e.g. James Bond, or being paid to get a job done e.g. Vincent in *Collateral*.

DON'T WANT CHANGE

There are times where the protagonist appears happy as they are. John Wick is happily retired until someone steals his car and kills his dog (*John Wick*). Woody loves being the *de facto* top toy (*Toy Story*). He doesn't want things to change. Ruben has everything he wants: a cool motor home, a girlfriend, and being a drummer in a band. But Woody and Ruben both get a rude awakening. Their lives are upturned, and they will fight to return things to the way there were, for as long as they can, until their will is broken and they realise that change is for the better.

WANT KNOWLEDGE

Mostly the domain of the detective, these protagonists want knowledge to solve a mystery. From Poirot to Holmes to Le Blanc, they're on the hunt for a criminal. They tend to be unusual characters with little back story. They rarely go through any internal change. If they did, would they be able to solve another murder? They don't live on past glories and move onto a new case. There are exceptions.

In *Se7en*, Somerset and Mills, follow a series of clues related to the seven sins to find a serial killer. When they fail to stop the antagonist in time, it ends in tragedy. When Detective Park Doo-man fails to find the killer in *Memories of Murder*, he's no longer a detective and haunted by his failure. In *Midnight Mass*, Riley Flynn, wants to know why God chose to let him live but not his passenger when he was drunk-driving. Unable to find an answer, he becomes an atheist, then sacrifices himself to protect a woman he loves.

At the beginning of a story, what your protagonist wants should be clear, specific, and something that is logical in the context of the character and the story world. If we emphasise with them, we'll want to see if our protagonist gets what they want. We'll want to see how they'll persist when their goal is threatened.

THE PRIZE METHOD

Figure 20: The Prize Method.

Now that you've decided what your protagonist wants, it can be helpful to consider it from different perspectives. Imagine you're viewing a second-hand car, you'd inspect it from every angle. Let's do that for the object of our protagonist's desire. For visual purposes, I'm calling this the Prize Method (Figure 20). It works best with a physical object but can work in all scenarios.

By answering the questions above, it will help you develop your story. Let's look at a completed example, using *Raiders of the Lost Ark* (Figure 21).

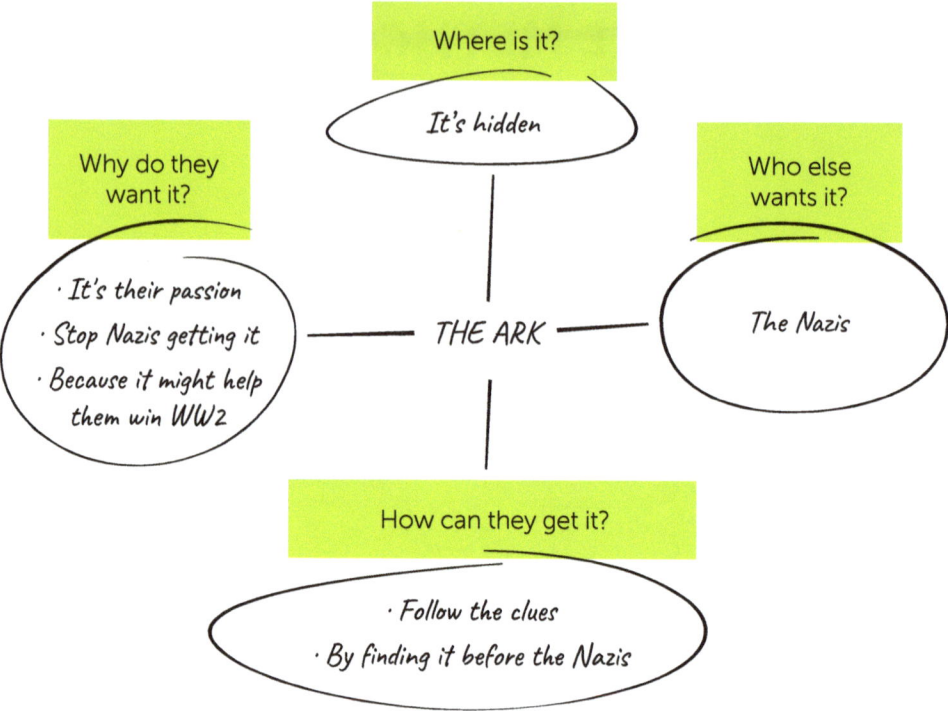

Figure 21: The Prize Method (*Raiders of the Lost Ark*).

We've now established what our protagonist wants: change, no change, or knowledge. We've also considered who or what might stop them from getting it, along with a rough plan of how they might achieve their goal, using The Prize Method. So let's move into the next phase after Want: Do.

DO

Having established what our protagonist wants, we now need to make it happen. For Woody, it's to rescue Buzz or lose the respect of the other toys (*Toy Story*). In all cases, this will be harder than it seems and in some, impossible. Now that our protagonist has his main objective, they've got to move forwards. In *Little Miss Sunshine*, Olive's family must travel to the West Coast so that she can perform in the pageant. For Ruben in *Sound of Metal*, it's to drive to a deaf community. Luke must take R2-D2 and C-3PO to Alderaan (*Star Wars: Episode IV: A New Hope*).

This journey section becomes the bulk of your story. The filling in your 3-Act sandwich. And it must challenge your protagonist. The journey in itself may form the majority of locations and interactions e.g. *Little Miss Sunshine*, *Bullet Train*, or *Compartment Number 6*. But more often, they visit one or more new places. These new environments bring opportunities for new experiences, friendships, and conflict. But they'll keep doing things to try to reach their main objective, completing smaller objectives to get closer to it. Your protagonist will have success and failures and will usually be changed be each. They'll eventually reach the Midpoint of the story, where they've become someone quite different, often the opposite of who they were at the start.

I'll discuss the Midpoint in more detail later but it's a 'pivot point' in the story. Our hero is transformed. Ruben changes from a noisy rebel to a calm team player. Luke masters the Force. Richard realises his dream of being an author is over while Olive is now brimming with confidence. Woody rallies the troops to rescue Buzz, rather than to feed his ego. With their new persona, our protagonist can tackle the remainder of Act 2 with confidence.

In terms of the three change scenarios our protagonist might start from, this will affect what they do:

1. **Want Change:** they'll act to get the change they want. If it's to win a sporting match e.g. *Rocky*, they'll train for it. If they want to change society, they'll start a crusade e.g. *Suffragette*
2. **Don't Want Change:** they'll do all they can to return their life to normal. For Ruben, this is to have a cochlear implant
3. **Want Knowledge:** they'll perform research, interview people, and look for clues

In their post Midpoint persona, they'll persevere to the end of Act 2, where they'll face a crisis*. After they recover, they enter, Act 3.

GET

In the third Act we discover whether our protagonist gets what they wanted. They began by wanting something and did everything they could to get it. The outcome appears binary – they either get it or don't. But stories are more complicated than that. As well as the external journey (**want**) they also have an internal journey (**need**). If the protagonist gets both what they want and what they need, it can feel undeserved if they've not undergone a significant set of challenges and been changed by them. If they've not grown as a person, we'll feel cheated if they achieve their (super) objective. That's why the Heart Plot – their emotional journey – is as essential as the Mind Plot. I'll go into the Heart Plot in more detail later, but as a quick test, use Table 7 to evaluate your protagonist's emotional journey.

---

* I'll cover this in more detail in the Hero's Journey section.

	ACT 1	ACT 2	ACT 3
Emotional State			

Table 7: Emotional Journey.

Dorothy's emotional journey in the *Wizard of Oz* is shown below (Table 8).

	ACT 1	ACT 2	ACT 3
Emotional State	☹️ Sadness	😮 Fear	🙂 Happiness

Table 8: Dorothy's Emotional State (*Wizard of Oz*).

Dorothy is sad after she's been whisked away from home. She travels through some scary places before finding a way to get back to Kansas. This table is a little simplistic as Dorothy goes through far more emotional states than the three listed above. However, it's a helpful summary of the inner journey she goes through. At the end of your story, you should know whether your protagonist got what they wanted and needed. Dorothy did find somewhere more colourful than life on the farm but realised there's, 'no place like home'.

The list of possible outcomes are:

1. They get what they want and what they need
2. They get what they want but not what they need
3. They don't get what they want, but they do get what they need
4. They don't get what they want or what they need

In most *Hollywood* endings the protagonist gets number 1. If the physical and emotional journey has been arduous and stepwise, this is a satisfying and cathartic result. Sometimes the character doesn't need anything. James Bond gets the girl, saves the world, and is mostly untroubled by any of it. Outcome 2, where the protagonist gets what they want but not what they need, these feel like hollow victories. Our hero is glad they've won, but we feel (even if they don't) that they've deluded themselves that this is their best outcome. They've achieved their objectives, but remained unchanged as a person. In *The Good Boss*, the protagonist Blanco, is anything but an exemplary employer. He achieves his goal of winning an award without correcting his errant behaviour. Although victorious, he pollutes everything and everyone around him.

Many stories, particularly arthouse films, exhibit outcome 3: our hero gets what they need but not what they want. This outcome is bittersweet but often feels like the right outcome, particularly if we're convinced the protagonist misjudged what was the most important thing to fix in their lives. In *Sound of Metal*, Ruben doesn't get to play the drums again, but finds inner peace. Option 4, where they achieve neither outcome, is rare. In *Memories of Murder*, Park Doo-Man doesn't get what he wants – the killer – or what he needs – to believe in logic, because he refuses to give up his misguided faith in his psychic power.

That covers the definitions of Want, Do, and Get, and how it relates to the three Acts of a story. Let's turn our attention to something that arises from a story being told in three parts.

WORLDS

The protagonist's story is a journey where they move from their world, through one or more others and finish in the antagonist's world. I will refer to these three groups as:

1. Home World
2. Alien World(s)
3. Shadow World

The protagonist begins the story in their **Home World**, often at work or following their passion. Life appears to be going well. But something happens that upsets the *status quo*, and they'll want to fix it. This will require them to leave their Home World and travel to one that's foreign to them, the **Alien World**. Sometimes this new world is distant, and they will need to travel to get there. Perhaps through a rabbit hole or via a tornado.

When they arrive in the Alien World, most of it will be strange to them, like the first day at school. They'll need to learn how to behave and navigate it. Their naivety may expose them to ridicule and danger. Run-ins with the locals are a standard feature. But they adapt, perhaps through the help of a mentor, or friends, and become, if not a master of the Alien World, comfortable. The Alien World doesn't have to be a new planet or location, and in some genres, e.g. action or sci-fi, they often visit several.

Finally, they enter the world of their antagonist, the **Shadow World**. This is darker and more dangerous than anywhere previously visited. It's the end of their journey and when they must face their antagonist. The Shadow World if often physically darker e.g. the Upside Down in *Stranger Things*, but it doesn't have to be e.g. *Midsommer*. Here's some example sets:

Star Wars: Episode IV: A New Hope

- **Home World:** Tatooine
- **Alien Worlds:** Anchorhead, Alderaan (destroyed)
- **Shadow World:** Death Star

Sound of Metal

- **Home World:** a recreational vehicle
- **Alien World:** Joe's rehabilitation centre
- **Shadow World:** Lou's father's flat in Paris

No Time to Die

- **Home World:** Jamaica
- **Alien Worlds:** Cuba, a prison, Norway
- **Shadow World:** World War II base on an island

Madagascar

- **Home World:** New York City's Central Park Zoo
- **Alien World:** Madagascar
- **Shadow World:** land of the predators

Brian and Charles

- **Home World:** empty farmhouse
- **Alien World:** Charles arrives
- **Shadow World:** Eddie's farmstead

From the examples above, you can see plenty of room for variation. The Home World can be anywhere you imagine your protagonist living. In *Star Wars: Episode IV: A New Hope*, Luke (like Dorothy in *The Wizard of Oz*) is stuck on a farm. When Luke travels to the chaotic port town of Anchorhead, it's very different from his peaceful moisture farm. For Ruben (*Sound of Metal*), it's somewhere quiet. When it comes to James Bond, a seasoned traveller, only the most exotic locations can push him out of his comfort zone. *Madagascar* cleverly plays with our expectations. You'd imagine that zoo animals might be fine when returned to their natural habitat. But the first Act establishes that these animals have become so institutionalised they're unsuited to living in the wild.

In *Brian and Charles*, we've a good example of a film that's nearly a single location. Shy Brian lives alone on a farmstead. He's doing okay, tinkering in his shed, but he'd like a companion. So, he builds one – Charles – an energetic, unruly child – which upturns his world. I expect a lot of new parents can attest to this reality. Brian's everyday existence will never be the same. He's gained a child rather than the mate he was hoping for. But Brian deals with the challenges of parenthood, until a neighbour kidnaps Charles. Brian overcomes his cowardliness and uses his prowess for invention to defeat the bully in the Shadow World.

In *Nope*, our horse training heroes are stuck in a single location. Their sedate world is upset by the arrival of the UFO or UAP (Unexplained Aerial Phenomena) which turns their Home World into an Alien World. It drops things from the sky, people and objects going missing, and electronics cut out. The move from Act 2 to Act 3 happens when OJ concludes that the saucer has claimed their homestead as its own. They're now in the Shadow World. At one point quite literally when it hovers above the house. Unable to tame it 'like a horse', they're forced to kill it and reclaim their home. Looking at your story through the lens of Worlds can help delineate and differentiate your Acts.

Worlds can also play a roll in shaping or defining a series. The streamers, such as Amazon Video and Netflix, have funded a large number of TV shows in recent years. While many have lasted one series, with a few lasting multiple e.g. *Game of Thrones*, the current numbers seems to be averaging out at three or four e.g. *Succession*, *Barry*. While this may be for a number of reasons: audience drop off, actors or writers wanting to move onto new projects, it does give an opportunity to analyse whole series in terms of Acts or in Worlds. As an example, the series *GLOW*, can be summarised as:

- **Home World:** a semi-derelict warehouse
- **Alien World:** a new ring with professional lighting
- **Shadow World:** Las Vegas

Having given an overview of plot, let's now focus on the Mind Plot.

NOTES

05.

THE MIND PLOT

The Mind Plot describes what our protagonist does. It's an external manifestation of the decisions they make based on how they're feeling at the time. If our character has no feelings, they will make the same decisions in each situation. As drama is about the human condition, feelings are paramount. And as stories are about change, the way our protagonist feels about the world should evolve and consequently, they'll behave differently over time. These alterations will occur through the outcomes of the obstacles they face and the choices they make in how to tackle them.

There are four types of obstacles:

1. Physical
2. Emotional
3. Organic
4. Fabricated

An obstacle might be physical e.g. a wall to climb, a maze to negotiate, emotional e.g. leaving home, proposing marriage; organic e.g. face a fear, reach a final of a competition; or fabricated e.g. a ticking bomb, a hostage is taken.

Multiple obstacles, of different types, will add variation and richness to your story. Using the four categories can help you do this. The second Act is where most of the obstacles reside, and it can be a challenge to create enough of them. Another way to generate obstacles is to consider who or what might put them in the protagonist's way other than the primary antagonist:

- Family
- Work colleagues
- The environment e.g. weather
- Rivals
- Institutions

If things have gone well and you've a long list of obstacles, you now need to arrange them in an order. The most obvious is by escalating difficulty. You'd also want to avoid having several of the same type in a row. Another way to arrange them is to hang them onto structures like the Mind Plot, Heart Plot, or the most well known story structure – the Hero's Journey.

THE HERO'S JOURNEY

The most discussed tool in screenwriting is the **Hero's Journey**. If you're already comfortable with it, that's great. This section is for those who aren't or need a refresher.

The academic Joseph Campbell coined the term Hero's Journey to describe a typical order of events he'd observed when studying ancient stories. Through his research, he found that a single main character – the hero, who could take many guises, would undergo the same trials and tribulations on an epic journey. He called this a monomyth. It was adopted by writers including George Lucas and Stephen Spielberg, and their success amplified its use in Hollywood. Subsequent authors have modernised it, e.g. Christopher Vogler, or added to it, e.g. Blake Snyder, and multiple interpretations are now available.

Before we dive into mine, let's talk through the limitations of the original:

- It's based on a selected pool of stories
- It's led by a single male
- It was popularised by Hollywood with its inherent Western biases
- Stories using it can feel formulaic

Although Joseph Campbell researched widely, it was always going to be constrained by the amount of material any one person could get access to, and read. In addition, when creating a universal formula, it's inevitable that less frequent but equally valid motifs are lost. While the Hero's Journey remains the most popular shorthand for screenwriters, there are several other significant texts I want to look at. The first two are the Bible's depiction of Jesus's life and *The Pilgrim's Progress*.

The Bible's New Testament

Jesus was born around 4 BC, lived to 30-33 BC, and is one of history's most well-known figures. His life is summarised below as a mixture of historically accurate and disputed events or facts.

- Born in Galilee in a Jewish family
- Visited by shepherds and three wise men who bring gifts
- Became a carpenter
- Father dies
- Baptised and taught by John the Baptist
- Travels to the Judaean Desert and fasts for forty days
- Tempted by the devil
- Jesus returns to Galilee
- Starts his ministry and appoints twelve apostles
- Gives healings, tells parables, and performs miracles
- Angers the authorities
- Has a meal with his disciples (The Last Supper)
- Betrayed by Judas or accepts imprisonment
- Taken by the authorities
- Crucified. He refuses painkillers. Rises from the dead
- A new religion is borne

If I summarise it as prose:

A special child is born. He grows up and takes up his father's career. Their father dies, and they meet an enigmatic mentor who teaches them a new, more elevated activity, that they were born to do. As part of their training, they must go on a journey and overcome a terrible ordeal. Once they've come face-to-face with the darkest version of themselves, they return home transformed. They launch a popular crusade, espousing a kinder and fairer method of living. People rally to the cause. This threatens the authorities, so they plan to stop him. The man and his friends have a private meal together where he's betrayed by one of them. The authorities arrive. The leader surrenders to avoid bloodshed. He's imprisoned, tortured, and left for dead. But he recovers briefly and inspires the world.

I suspect you can already see how Jesus's life is similar to mythical heroes e.g. Luke Skywalker, Paul Atreides (*Dune*) and Harry Potter. Their heritage, e.g. Luke's father being a Jedi, predisposes them to greatness. Jesus was the son of God. Some find these story elements unrealistic and uninspiring. But if genetics continue to play a part in social mobility, their use will still resonate. And Jesus always remained humble, never proclaiming he was a hero – another common motif.

The story of Jesus has two other elements worth highlighting: the first is his **resurrection**. Often utilised in genre stories, it's visually and emotionally exhilarating: the hero is out for the count but somehow pulls themselves upright for one last fight. Examples include the reboot of the T-100 in *Terminator: Judgment Day* or Batman's self-injection of a green serum in *The Batman*.

Jesus's life is also a story of **redemption**. American culture is well known for its ability to forgive past failures (particularly in business) and offer second chances. Jesus lived a sinless life and died for our sins, for which he's repaid by being brought back from the dead and ascending to heaven.

The Pilgrim's Progress

The Pilgrim's Progress is a Christian allegory written by the Baptist minister and preacher John Bunyan, while he was in prison for refusing not to hold any more services (in defiance of Charles II).

- The protagonist, Christian, is an ordinary man
- He's troubled and leaves the family home looking for the Celestial City
- An Evangelist directs him on his way

- Christian falls into the Slough of Despond and sinks under the weight of his sins, but he pulls himself out
- Three men tempt Christian from his route but the Evangelist intervenes
- Christian has his burdens removed
- Three angels give Christian a scroll to enter the Celestial City
- Christian loses the scroll and then recovers it
- Christian meets a porter who helps him avoid being eaten by lions
- Christian rests in the House of the Palace Beautiful and is given armour
- Christian battles and defeats a dragon
- Christian crosses the Valley of the Shadow of Death
- Christian enters a city of debauchery but avoids temptation
- Christian is joined by another traveller called Hopeful. They're offered a bribe to stop, but refuse
- They take a shortcut and are captured by a Giant who tortures them. They escape
- A false angel fools them but a real one rescues them
- Christian and Hopeful pass through an Enchanted Ground (it makes them sleepy)
- They approach the Celestial City[5]
- A traveller called Ignorance enters without a scroll and is sent to hell
- Christian and Hopeful cross the River of Death and enter the Celestial City

---

5. Perhaps inspiration for *The Wizard of Oz* where our heroes succumbed to a soporific poison before reaching the Emerald City.

Let's rewrite it as prose:

A man who feels guilt for things he's done in his life decides that moving to a new city will give him a new lease on life. His family stays behind, but he leaves anyway, weighed down by guilt. On his journey, he's joined by other travellers and overcomes several challenges. He reaches a safe house and becomes free from sinful feelings. Someone gives him a key to enter the city he's heading for. He faces more challenges, including lions, a dragon, a bribe, a giant, trickery, poison, and evil. Finally, he crosses a dangerous river and enters the grand city.

The Pilgrim's Progress has a strong focus on Act 2 with a multitude of obstacles for Christian to overcome. It's similar to *Don Quixote* or other stories with a marathon adventurer such as Sinbad, Indiana Jones, Bruce Banner, or James Bond. These heroes travel to multiple locations and face a variety of mythological or physical adversaries. These are also films where the hero has accomplices, not all of whom may survive.

At the Midpoint of *The Pilgrim's Progress*, Christian goes from guilt-ridden to guilt-free. The guilt he carried made him vulnerable (sinking in the pit) and is a common character trait in many other protagonists. In *The Peanut Butter Falcon*, Tyler feels guilt for the part he played in the death of his brother. In *The Lost Daughter*, Leda feels remorse for her choices as a mother. And in *Eleanor Oliphant is Completely Fine*, Eleanor carries the pain of not being able to save her sister.

Let's now look at what is regarded as one of the four great classical novels of Chinese literature: *Journey to the West*. This was published in the sixteenth century and was reworked into the TV series, *Monkey*. Set during the Tang Dynasty, it tells the story of the pilgrimage of a Buddhist monk called Xuanzang (in the TV series, Tripitaka). He travels through the Asian and Indian continents to gather sacred texts and return with them. To summarise:

- Tripitaka is disappointed that the South has become hedonistic and sinful
- He decides to travel with his disciples, including the violent Monkey, to the West to fetch a religious manual
- They set off and find themselves in rough terrain, inhabited by demons and animal spirits
- They discover the occasional safe refuge
- Tripitaka is often captured, then rescued by his disciples (one of which is a horse)
- They fight off numerous attacks and reach Vulture Peak
- Tripitaka gets the scriptures, and the disciples are rewarded

So like Jesus, we have a protagonist who believes the world could be better than it is. On Tripitaka's journey, his accomplices are part human-part animal, a common motif in fantasy or sci-fi stories e.g. *Guardians of the Galaxy*. Like Christian, they also have a final dramatic destination, although Vulture Peak sounds more intimidating than the Celestial City.

The other classic Chinese novels are *Romance of the Three Kingdoms*, *Water Margin*, and *Dream of the Red Chamber*. *Romance of the Three Kingdoms* by Luo Guanzhong tells the story of feudal lords and their families who fought for control of the remnants of the Han dynasty. This feels like a blueprint for stories about warring factions, be they military or political. *The Water Margin* describes a hundred outlaws who rebelled against the government, were granted amnesty, then switched sides to face invading forces. Elements of this are seen in films like *Assault on Precinct 13*, or *Suicide Squad*.

Jin Ping Mei is a spin-off from *Water Margin* and focusses on Ximen Qing, a wealthy merchant, and his household of wives and concubines. This setup is replicated in *Big Love* or *Sister Wives*. Finally, *Dream of the Red Chamber* follows the rise and decline of a family headed by a powerful father, much like *The Sopranos* or *Succession*.

The last few stories lack a physical journey. The drama is concentrated on inter-personal conflict within a mostly singular location. The redemption element is also absent. The characters go through ups and downs but return to their old ways. Just like a sitcom. In *The Sopranos*, Tony seeks help for his behaviour, but never entirely goes straight. There's also a more significant presence of women, sex and humour in these more static stories. They're more focussed on local conflicts, with known antagonists, rather than the mysteries of a quest.

Before we dive deeper into the Hero's Journey, we should pause to discuss William Shakespeare's influence on storytelling. As well as his 5-Act structures, most of his stories were not redemptive or transformative but like the Chinese examples, were often based on historical events. Many of his plays have tragic endings. His approach lends itself well to TV, which has the time to delve into the psyche of complex, often dark figures and worlds e.g. *Breaking Bad, Game of Thrones*.

So, when designing your plot, you've now got plenty of other templates to utilise. Nonetheless, the Hero's Journey remains the dominant template. Here's my summary of it:

A character finds their comfortable world upended by a mysterious foe. They feel compelled to do something to repair it. They leave home with or without comrades and are given guidance. They confront physical and mental challenges. They receive help but may also be betrayed. They face a tragedy but reach their final destination, where their oppressor resides. They battle them and are nearly overcome. But they gather their physical strength, conquer their fears, and defeat their opponent, achieving their ultimate goal. They return home, rewarded.

Let's go through the Hero's Journey in more depth.

ACT 1

In an earlier section, I previewed the Hero's Journey using the skeleton document. Now, I'll go through it in more detail. Not all stories use every step listed or position them in this order. And as you've just seen, many stories don't use it all.

HOME WORLD

We begin with the protagonist in their Home World. This is the first of three worlds they'll encounter. This environment should feel safe, and they must look fairly comfortable here. This doesn't mean it has to be objectively calm and peaceful. If your protagonist's a demon, they might feel at home in a burning pit of fire. It's good to bear in mind that whatever the world is that you've chosen, the protagonist will be doing something that feels natural within it. At this point, we're probably not consciously aware that something's wrong. They seem at home.

STATUS QUO

Our protagonist follows their typical routine — doing their job, their passion or just being themselves, comfortable with life. But there may just be a hint that they're a round peg in a square hole. Perhaps they're overly zealous, like Woody in *Toy Story*, organising the other toys, or Ruben in *Sound of Metal*, smashing the skins like an animal. Or they look a little out of place, like Ruby on the fishing boat in *Coda*, a girl singing alone in a harsh, noisy environment. In *Russian Doll*, Nadia appears to be in her element — at her birthday party with her friends, smoking and drinking. But she behaves more like an observer than as a participant, never standing still. Often on the first viewing of this moment, everything appears okay. However, if you rewatch it, you'll observe a chink in their armour.

DARK CLOUDS

The next step can be as subtle as the previous one. There's an indication that the protagonist's safe world is under threat. Dark clouds are on the horizon and they will eventually have to investigate. In *Toy Story*, Woody's worried that they might get replaced, unless everything is shipshape for Andy's birthday. In *Russian Doll*, Nadia worries about her future (she mentions her age) and what is that strange artwork on the back of the bathroom door? For genre movies like fantasy or horror, it's often a jump scare. In *Get Out*, they hit a deer while driving.

FLAW EXPOSED

Early on, we'll observe our protagonist's flaw. It's something that makes their life harder. Their flaw is linked to an inner need that prevents them from making the most of what they could be. In *Russian Doll*, Nadia drinks, smokes, and takes drugs. She reveals that she's lived to be older than her mother — her self-destructive behaviour is linked to this loss. In *Toy Story*, Woody's insecurity about being replaced drives his determination to make Andy's party a success. Ruben's stubbornness means he keeps playing even when he can't hear. In *Coda*, Ruby's flaw is her selflessness, taking on many tasks for her deaf family at the expense of her passion for singing.

The flaw doesn't have to be objectively good or bad, just something that prevents the protagonist from reaching their potential. For Andrew in *Whiplash*, his devotion to his family stops him from becoming a great drummer.

SAVE THE CAT

Popularised by Blake Snyder, the Save the Cat moment is when the protagonist does something we find empathetic. Their action must be selfless, i.e., it should provide no benefit to the protagonist (and might even be somewhat negative). As its regular inclusion has become something of an in-joke for writers, you'll often have actual cats saved, be it Nadia searching for hers or Nathan Drake giving Sully a cat in *Uncharted*.

You can be more subtle. Elliot blackmails a stranger to give him his maltreated dog (*Mr Robot*), and in *Three Billboards Outside Epping, Missouri*, Mildred turns over a cockroach stuck on its back. In *Toy Story*, Woody saves Bo Peep's sheep. In *Coda*, Ruby takes her parents to see a doctor about their jock itch and Danny gives water to a neighbour's thirsty dog (*The Karate Kid*). Whatever the action is, remember to make it selfless.

INCITING INCIDENT

The Inciting Incident is the moment when everything changes for the protagonist. This unexpected event upends their world to such an extent, they have no option but to respond. But as their flaw is still in place, they'll not take the right course of action just yet. In *Toy Story*, Buzz Lightyear arrives. In *Russian Doll*, Nadia gets run over by a car and reappears back at her party, alive and well. Ruben loses his hearing. These are dramatic interruptions, and they need to be.

Our hero has been living their flawed life without consequences. We all have flaws, and rarely do we fix them. We go about our daily activities, often unaware that our imperfections are holding us back. A missed promotion, a love affair not realised. Buzz's arrival is a bolt from the blue, threatening Woody's position as Andy's favourite toy. Woody saw himself as the natural leader, and here is someone who's trained to go into space. Ruben's life revolves around music. He's the drummer in the band with his girlfriend. What happens if he can no longer play?

An Inciting Incident surprises our protagonist and threatens their future.

ANTAGONIST

Early on in the story, we should get a sense of who or what the antagonist is because they're usually responsible for the Inciting Incident. In some cases, this is obvious, like the first shark attack in *Jaws*. In other cases, particularly a murder mystery, the killer's unknown, even if their handiwork is evident. But they quite often appear briefly e.g. *See How They Run*. In *Bodyguard*, David persuades a woman not to commit a terrorist bombing, not realising she's the mastermind. (In some stories, the antagonist will openly taunt the protagonist e.g. in *Chinatown* or when Kingpin threatens Daredevil). A strong connection between the antagonist and the Inciting Incident strengthens the story by making the final confrontation more meaningful.

The more you hide the antagonist's appearance, the greater the suspense created e.g. *Wizard of Oz*, *Cloverfield*, *Monsters*. In *Jaws*, the shark remains mostly invisible for the first two-thirds of the film. This can create mystery too e.g. in *Russian Doll*, is the weirdness caused by the strange art form on the back of the bathroom door? Or the fact the building was a Jewish school? Or is it Allan – the drunk man in the shop? These questions create a mystery that Nadia (and the viewer) needs to solve. Not all characters that trigger the Inciting Incident must **remain** antagonists. In *Toy Story*, Buzz begins as Woody's antagonist but they're friends by the end.

BAD BEHAVIOUR

At this point in the Hero's Journey, our protagonist might do something hasty to try to return things to normal. There must be a quick fix, surely? It's brief, awful, and driven by our hero's flaw. Woody pushes Buzz off the dresser. Nadia sits on the edge of a bridge, late at night, and topples over backwards. Ruben plays drums despite being told not to. It's a desperate, lazy attempt by our protagonist, that one suspects even they realise is a bad idea. It doesn't work.

COLD FEET

Our protagonist is now aware there's something wrong, and their sticking plaster hasn't worked. Buzz falls out of the window rather than just getting stuck behind the dresser. Ruben can't stay in time with Lou. Our would be hero realises that a more considered action is needed. But they get cold feet when given the offer of adventure. Nadia **tells** the universe that she refuses to engage in its manipulations. Woody won't help find Buzz. In *Star Wars: Episode VII - The Force Awakens,* Rey refuses to take Luke's light sabre and runs away.

As the task is so daunting, it shouldn't be surprising that our protagonist isn't keen. In *Don Quixote*, our titular hero leaves home, changes his mind, and goes back. (But don't worry, he gets back on his horse and heads out for an additional 1,000 pages of adventures). This fear of the unknown endears them to us, creating further empathy for our hero.

LEAVE HOME

Our protagonist now gets further encouragement to leave their Home World. Nadia dies a few more times. Rey is chased through the forest. Often called 'three pushes and a nudge', our protagonist finally realises that staying put is not realistic. If you think about our hesitancy to do something new, e.g. an interview, driving test, or the first day at a new job, is it any surprise our hero is anxious?

Sometimes our protagonist leaves without choosing to e.g. Alice down a rabbit hole (*Alice's Adventures in Wonderland*) or Dorothy getting whisked away to Oz. But most often, they'll choose to leave. Woody climbs out of Andy's bedroom, Nadia tiptoes out of the party, and Ruben drives to the retreat. Tied into their decision to go is an **objective**. Woody's is to bring Buzz back (or at least appear like he tried to). Ruben has to learn sign language, in order to play the drums with his girlfriend. They all **want** something, and this first objective is what they hope will return things to normal.

These 10 stages of the Hero's Journey occupy the first Act. It's a lot of stuff to pack into the first 20% of your movie. In *Toy Story*, Buzz falls out the window after 26 minutes. In *Russian Doll*, it's the whole of the first episode (25 minutes).

ACT 2

Act 2 is all about obstacles and how our protagonist is transformed by their attempts to overcome them.

ALIEN WORLD

We now enter a new and Alien World. This reality is somewhere completely different for our protagonist. For Woody, he's outside without Andy. For Nadia, it's a world where she knows that if she dies, she'll come back to life. *Russian Doll* is a good example where the protagonist doesn't move to a new geography but where the Home World itself is transformed. It's more common in sci-fi or horror. In *Jaws*, the shark's arrival makes a safe, seaside town a death trap.

In this new world, our protagonist needs to learn its rules and norms of behaviour. In *Toy Story*, Buzz needs to learn how to be a toy. At first, he doesn't believe he is one. So, when Woody plays dead when humans appear, Buzz doesn't. Our protagonist will observe new things in this fresh environment, make friends and encounter enemies. When Luke enters the cantina in *Star Wars: Episode IV - A New Hope*, he nervously studies the various life forms before heading to the bar. This environment is very different from his quiet farmstead. Woody and Buzz meet the aliens in the grabber, Sid's mutilated toys as well as his dog, Scud. Nadia meets up with her frosty workmates, her drug dealer, and Allan. However, there is one person, above all others, that can help them the most: a mentor.

MENTOR

At this point, if our protagonist has not already met a mentor, they'll often get help from an experienced advisor. This person could be a friend, or the classic wise, older man (Gandalf, Mr Miyagi). But it doesn't have to be. In *True Blood*, the wisest vampire is the oldest living one but Godrich was young when he was converted. In the TV series *The Queen's Gambit*, a different character performs the role of mentor in each episode. As Beth progresses up through the chess ranks and gets older, she needs tailored advice, best given by different people. In some stories there isn't a mentor, making the journey for the protagonist harder.

Before the quest begins, the mentor will tell our hero the secret to succeeding in their mission. But the protagonist will ignore this advice. In *Lord of the Rings: The Fellowship of the Ring*, when Frodo wishes he hadn't agreed to take the ring, Gandalf tells him, 'So do all that live to see such times but that is not for them to decide. All we have to decide is what to do with the time that is given to us.' Mike tells Nadia to be more careful when she nearly falls down a flight of steps. Woody tells the other toys, 'It doesn't matter how much we're played with. What matters is that we're here for Andy when he needs us. That's what we're made for. Right?'. Joe tells Ruben he needs to heal what's **in** his head, not what's on each side (i.e. his ears).

FRIENDS AND ENEMIES

In Act 2, our protagonist makes some friends and encounters some adversaries. The friends can take many forms, such as a couple of droids (*Star Wars*) or a jovial police sergeant (*Die Hard*). This is your chance to introduce secondary characters that enrich the environment. They should be comfortable in the Alien World, knowing where things are and how things work. These new friends will advise and guide our protagonist and may accompany them on their journey. Near the end, whether by choice or circumstance, the hero will (at least initially) face the antagonist by themselves.

Act 2 is a good opportunity to introduce some lower tier enemies. The enemies can be conventional e.g. lackeys sent by the antagonist or random locals. How our protagonist copes with these assaults is up to you, but each choice should reveal something of their evolving character. So, while early on, their mentor might step in, as Obi-Wan does in the cantina, as our hero matures, they should too. Being busy is vital here. If they're too passive, something levelled at Jyn in *Rogue One: A Star Wars Story*, it can feel that their friends (or the enemy's failings) are doing all the hard work, and they're progressing more through luck than judgement.

MIDPOINT

As our protagonist moves through the Alien World, they grow in confidence. But their reluctance to address their flaw means things get progressively worse, despite any short-lived successes. Nadia refuses to be less selfish, so her world degrades. Buzz's refusal to accept he's a toy and Woody's antagonism toward him, hamper their attempts to get home. Ignoring their flaws won't make them go away and it all comes to a head at the Midpoint.

In a screenplay, the Midpoint is often dead centre, so on page 45 in a 90-page script. The Midpoint should be a complete shift in the story or our protagonist's character. It's an 180-degree turnaround or a point of no return. It takes two forms, the protagonist:

1. Becomes their opposite, or
2. Meets their opposite

Let's go through both options.

Becomes their Opposite

Frequently, our protagonist's changed so much that they've become their opposite. This change should feel genuine and earned and they should be noticeably different from the person they were in the beginning. In *The Godfather*, Michael arrives in the story a decorated soldier with no intention of joining the family business. But at the Midpoint, he kills two men in cold blood. He's moved from being a **legitimised** killer to an **unlawful** one. Buzz realises he's not a man but a toy.

These transformations are associated with events that can't be reversed. Michael cannot **unkill** those men just as Buzz cannot unknow he's a toy. Their conversions are psychological. They have a new mindset that changes their perception of who they are and possibly how others see them. For Buzz, Woody has always known that he's a toy, but for Michael's family, he's now truly one of them.

Stories are about change. It makes sense that our protagonist should undergo this at the Midpoint.

Meets their Opposite

The other type of Midpoint is for our protagonist to meet the mirror opposite of themselves. This person is often the antagonist, but not always. In *Russian Doll*, Nadia and Allan meet properly for the first time at the Midpoint. They're opposites: Nadia is white, female, reckless, and loves drugs. Alan is male, black, risk-averse and lives healthily. But despite being two completely different people from each other, Nadia states, 'We are in this together'.

In *1917*, Blake and Schofield come face-to-face with a German soldier for the first time. At the Midpoint, the German pilot kills Blake, leaving Schofield alone. In *Knives Out*, the protagonist, Marta Cabrera, is rescued by the family she works for's errant son, who we find out later is the murderer. In *Goldfinger*, James Bond meets his nemesis, Auric, while strapped to a table, about to be cut in half by a laser.

Both types of Midpoints are forms of mirroring. The mirror image is either who they've become or the person they meet.

MOMENT OF REFLECTION

After the tumultuous event that is the Midpoint, there's a pause – a moment of relative calm. I call this the Moment of Reflection (MOR). At this point, our protagonist examines themself (Become their Opposite) or their opposite takes centre stage (Meet their Opposite). In the first scenario, it's as if the protagonist is giving himself (or the audience) time to adjust to their new self: **I'm now this. So what do I do?** For Michael, leaning back in a chair, it's to plan the family's next move. For Buzz, it's watching a TV advert and realising he's a toy – in this case, the Midpoint and MOR are combined.

For the Meet their Opposite Midpoints, their mirror image takes centre stage. Auric explains his dastardly plan. Hugh slurps a beer while telling Marta what she should do. When Blake lies dying, Schofield holds him in his arms. Allan smashes a mirror, demonstrating that the MOR doesn't always have to be a calm event.

In summary, at the Midpoint:

1. The protagonist becomes their opposite and reflects on themselves
2. The protagonist meets their opposite, who reflects on them

ANOTHER ALIEN WORLD

If your story is one of a globe-trekking spy, academic archaeologist, biblical puzzle solver, or a galaxy ranging team of misfits, you probably have at least one more Alien World to visit. Treat it as a separate Act or sub-Act, e.g. 2A, 2B. By doing this, you retain their link to Act 2 and all the typical elements it contains, but it keeps it as its own separate mini-story. This subset of Act 2 should have all the essential aspects of any Act. It should have a world with its rules of engagement and a beginning, middle, and end. Our protagonist should arrive at the new location, assess their whereabouts, and try to meet their next objective. They will have some failures and some successes before the end of our mini-Act, where they may or may not have achieved their short-term goal. Whatever the result, they'll be off to another Alien World or the Shadow World.

ULTIMATE TEST AND SIGNIFICANT DEATH

Towards the end of Act 2, our protagonist is navigating the world with confidence. And it's at this point, they face their most challenging moments to date. The Ultimate Test will happen along with the death (or end) of someone or something important (the Significant Death). These two events happen close together, just before Act 3. The protagonist might succeed in this Ultimate Test (UT), but it will feel like a hollow victory after a Significant Death (SD) occurs.

In *Terminator 2: Judgment Day*, our protagonists break into the heavily guarded Cyberdyne facility to destroy all the material related to the first T-800 (UT). Miles Dyson – a scientist studying them – is persuaded to help them into the building. As they plant explosive charges, the police arrive, and shoot Miles. He stays, holding the detonator, while the others escape. He is killed in the explosion

(SD). So, although they've succeeded, our heroes are responsible for someone's death, something John said shouldn't happen.

In *Little Miss Sunshine*, Richard confronts Stan Grossman, his route to publishing success, who informs him that there's no book deal and that he's a failure (UT). Richard returns to his family, crestfallen. The following day, his father, Edwin, dies (SD). In *The Godfather*, Michael fails to buy out Mo Greene (UT), who tells him that the Corleone family is weak. A few months later, Don Vito dies in his tomato garden (SD). In *Toy Story*, the other toys abandon Woody after he fails to convince them that he does really care about Buzz, who he's made up with (UT). Woody ends their friendship to save Buzz (SD).

In *Sound of Metal*, Ruben can stick with the retreat or have surgery. He undergoes surgery (UT) – which is successful, even if it's the 'wrong' choice – and sells the RV to pay for it (SD). In *Another Round*, with the impacts of heavy drinking becoming dangerous (UT), they agree to stop the experiment. But Tommy continues to drink and later dies (SD).

The Ultimate Test and Significant Death are two events, but like Laurel and Hardy; one cannot exist without the other.

ACT 3

We're now into Act 3, our shortest Act. In this Act, we accelerate to the end of the story. Stuff comes thick and fast. These are desperate times for our protagonist following the trauma of the Ultimate Test and Significant Death. Everything the protagonist has done has brought them closer to getting what they want, but they're not there yet and their inner need is still not met. Our protagonist usually looks or behaves differently going into the final Act. Ruben can hear (sort of) and his head is shaven. Martin is sober (but separated). Ruby has an audition for Berklee (*Coda*). Buzz now freezes when humans appear.

SHADOW WORLD

In their new form, they're ready to enter the demon's lair: the Shadow World. This is scarier and more dangerous than anywhere they've been before. It doesn't have to be a dark, black cavern, but that's a common trope. Perhaps because most of us feared the dark as children. The key thing is that the Shadow World should be where the antagonist feels most at home. It's 'their' domain, and they know best how it operates. They're on home turf with home advantage.

The protagonist will be uneasy entering the Shadow World but must keep going, swiping away metaphorical or real cobwebs. Sometimes a character will bar their way. This could be anything from a three-headed dog to a wardrobe-sized bouncer. Once inside, our protagonist will take in their new environment and move towards the antagonist.

ALL OR NOTHING

In this next stage, our protagonist has come so far; they've nothing to lose. They're far from home and have made multiple sacrifices on their journey. Their unresolved flaw has made things much more difficult and now, they're ready to address it. The All or Nothing moment may not be successful. For Woody and Buzz, it's to work together. Ruben asks Lou's father's for money to buy back the van so he and Lou can go back on the road. As someone who didn't have a relationship with his father, this is a big step for Ruben and his last chance to reset his life.

In *Another Round*, Martin won't talk about his feelings, but opens up to his wife, when he's got nothing to lose. In *Terminator 2: Judgment Day*, the T-800 sacrifices himself to save John and his mother. In *Russian Doll*, with almost all of their friends and possessions gone, and Nadia and Allan dying repeatedly, Nadia admits to Ruth that, as a child, she asked to be taken away from her mother, which she believes led to her suicide. Allan tells Beatrice he knew about her affair all along and that he's felt like a failure for a long time, making him suicidal.

In these moments, our protagonists reveal their deepest wounds and, in doing so, unburden themselves just in time for the Final Fight.

SUIT UP

Before they face the antagonist, our hero needs to get ready for the battle. They must Suit Up. Here are some examples:

- **Sound of Metal:** Ruben shaves off his hair and puts on a beanie
- **Another Round:** Martin tidies himself up before lunch with his wife
- **Jerusalem:** Jonny puts on a suit before the Council employees arrive
- **Aliens:** Ripley loads her guns
- **Russian Doll:** (new) Allan wears a red scarf, and (new) Nadia wears a white shirt
- **Good:** Professor Halder dresses in full Nazi regalia

FINAL FIGHT

In the Final Fight, our protagonist meets their antagonist. At this point, several different things happen in quick succession:

1. Out for the Count
2. Reborn
3. Special Move
4. Success

Our protagonist, on the verge of victory, is defeated (**Out for the Count**). They often fall to the floor or even die. But they pull themselves together or come back to life (**Reborn**). Then through an unexpected action (**Special Move**), they defeat their antagonist (**Success**), often in a surprising and elegant way. It can feel particularly satisfying if the **Special Move** is foreshadowed. Let's look at a few examples:

Toy Story

- **Out for the Count:** the match to light the rocket fuse is blown out. Woody cries on the ground
- **Reborn:** Woody realises Buzz's helmet is focusing the sun's rays. He jumps up
- **Special Move:** Woody directs the focussed sun rays onto the fuse. It lights
- **Success:** Woody and Buzz are launched into the air then glide safely into the family's car next to Andy

Sound of Metal

- **Out for the Count:** Ruben realises that their rock and roll lifestyle is not good for Lou's health. They go to sleep
- **Reborn:** Ruben wakes up and leaves the flat by himself
- **Special Move:** Ruben takes out his hearing aids and watches city life in silence
- **Success:** Ruben experiences a sacred stillness

Terminator 2: Judgment Day

- **Out for the Count:** the T-1000 skewers the T-800 to the floor and it powers off
- **Reborn:** the T-800 reroutes power and gets back up

- **Special Move:** the T-800 arrives unexpectedly and shoots the T-1000 with a grenade launcher
- **Success:** the T-1000 falls into a furnace and burns up

Another Round

- **Out for the Count:** Tommy lies in his coffin
- **Reborn:** Martin's wife, Anika, tells him she misses him
- **Special Move:** Martin dances with his friends among the graduating students
- **Success:** Martin's found the joy in life again

Russian Doll

- **Out for the Count:** Nadia and Allan die one more time
- **Reborn:** everything appears to be back to normal, but they've been reborn in separate timelines
- **Special Move:** (new) Allan stops (old) Nadia getting run over; (new) Nadia stops (old) Allan jumping off the roof
- **Success:** the two pairs enter a tunnel, and new (Allan) and new (Nadia) are reunited

Following this four-step combination, the protagonist has addressed their flaw and been successful. Even if this might lead to tragedy.

IT TAKES TWO

When you reach the Final Fight, you'll often find that the protagonist uses a mixture of both masculine and feminine traits to succeed. A sole protagonist might encompass both parts, but it's usually split between two characters. While breaking these actions via gender might feel outdated, they'll do for the purposes of this tool:

- **Masculine:** physical, e.g. fighting
- **Feminine:** non-physical, e.g. acts of kindness

Some examples:

- **Superman and Lois:** at the end of season 1, Clark and Lois face twin threats. Edge is at the mine with several minions while Zeta-Rho has taken over Jordan. Superman and Irons travel to the mine for a physical face-off (1), while Lois uses a mind-melding device to release her son (2)
- **I am Mother:** the heroine succeeds using a physical solution (threatens with a gun) and a non-physical one (talking)
- **Fleabag:** much of the conflict in this series is verbal. When needed, she employs (1) swearing or (2) vulnerability e.g. explaining what she's doing and why

OUTCOME

Following the Final Fight, you usually finish with the glow of success. But this success has not come without costs. The friends' experiment in *Another Round* led to Tommy's death. Allan is no longer suicidal, but Nadia can't promise he'll be happy either. The T-1000 is destroyed but so is the T-800. In *Toy Story*, Buzz and Woody land back in the car and are spotted by Andy, who's delighted to see them. All seems perfect until they discover that one of Andy's Christmas presents is a toy-chewing dog.

Most endings are bittersweet. In *Memento*, Leonard kills his wife's murderer, but we know he's mistaken, as he's in an endless loop. In the original *The Thing*, MacReady and Childs kill the alien, but realise that one of them could be infected.

In some films, the outcome may feel to us like a failure for the protagonist, but for them it may be a success. In *Whiplash*, Andrew abandons his family for the chance of fame. We may be disappointed by his choice but it's the right one for him. When

Gittes fails to save Evelyn and her daughter in *Chinatown*, it's a tragic ending. But it works within the movie's theme, that powerful people always get what they want. And after all, colleagues warned him not to go back to Chinatown.

Jack Nicholson's character in *One Flew over the Cuckoo's Nest*, also ignores warnings and is lobotomised. We may not feel he deserves this outcome, but the world he lives in makes it inevitable. In *Nightmare Alley*, we learn through flashbacks that Stanton is a cruel son and a trickster. His relegation to a circus freak feels deserved.

REWARD

After the dust has settled our protagonists may receive a reward for their achievements. Heroes like the Avengers are too humble to get a real prize, so make do with shwarma. In *Star Wars IV: A New Hope*, Han and Luke receive medals. In *Toy Story*, Mr Potato Head gets a Mrs Potato Head, and Woody receives a kiss from Bo Peep. In *Russian Doll*, their reward is being back together.

For most, merely returning their world to normal is a sufficient reward. They also addressed their flaw. The prize might be that they've changed others, e.g. *Forrest Gump* or that they changed the world, e.g. *Selma*, *Oppenheimer*.

If our protagonist is not already home, they may return home. If they've removed the threat to their home, e.g. *Jaws* or *Nope*, they don't have to go anywhere. But in other stories, they might need a route back, such as tapping their heels together (*Wizard of Oz*). In *The Queen's Gambit*, Beth decides that her home is with the Moscowvite chess players on the street, rather than a politically motivated tour.

Now the theory is clear, let's put the Hero's Journey into practice. I'll use the first episode of *The Queen's Gambit* to show how the Hero's Journey can work with a TV episode. But first, let's see how it maps to *Spirited Away*.

Spirited Away

This elegant Studio Ghibli production tells the story of Chihiro, forced to move to a new town by her parents, leaving her school and friends behind. Chihiro is upset by the change. Themes of greed and pollution run through the story. Before they reach their new house, they visit a derelict amusement park. Her mother tells her, 'It's fun to move to a new place, it's an adventure.'

But when her parents change into pigs, Chihiro must navigate the abandoned amusement park to reverse the spell, while also preventing herself from becoming a spirit. There are several object archetypes (more on this later): a farewell card, gold seal, and a purple hair band. *Spirited Away* has most of the elements of the Hero's Journey I've described but in a slightly different order:

ACT 1

- **Home World:** an abandoned amusement park near their new home
- **Status Quo:** Chihiro is a 10-year-old girl forced to move to a new town
- **Dark Clouds:** her flowers start to die and they drive past shrines that may contain spirits
- **Refusal:** Chihiro doesn't want to go through the tunnel into the park
- **Bad Behaviour:** in the park, she doesn't stay with parents and wanders off
- **Inciting Incident:** her parents become pigs
- **Antagonist:** Zambia might turn her into an animal
- **Flaw Exposed:** she's scared of being alone
- **Leave Home:** Chihiro must enter the bathhouse and get a job from Kamaji

ACT 2

- **Alien World:** a bathhouse for spirits where humans aren't welcome
- **Save the Cat:** she helps a squashed soot creature
- **Mentor:** Lin ('If you need anything, ask me')
- **Friends and Enemies:** Haku's a friend, and Kamaji states he's her grandfather
- **Midpoint:** Chihiro lets No-Face into the bathhouse, who consumes the staff
- **Ultimate Test and Significant Death:** Chihiro uses half the River Spirit's cake (that might cure her parents) to save Haku (who's close to death) and the other half for the lonely No-Face

ACT 3

- **Suit Up:** Chihiro changes from her bathhouse clothes into her original clothing
- **All or Nothing:** Chihiro travels by train to meet her antagonist using a one-way ticket
- **Shadow World:** Zeniba's home, Swamp Bottom
- **Out for the Count:** Chihiro remembers when she nearly drowned, but the current took her to safety. She realises this was Haku when he was a river spirit, Kohaku
- **Reborn:** with the knowledge of his old name, Haku is reborn
- **Final Fight:** Yubba tests Chihiro by asking her to choose which of the pigs are her parents
- **Special Move:** Chihiro realises that none of them are
- **Outcome:** her parents turn back into humans
- **Reward:** they get to their new home with Chihiro full of confidence

The Queen's Gambit, Episode 1

In this TV series, an orphaned girl, Elizabeth Harmon, becomes a chess prodigy, taking on the primarily male establishment. In the opening episode, our protagonist moves into an orphanage. The children are given tranquillisers to keep them sedated. Another girl, Jolene, advises Beth on life there. Beth asks the custodian, Shaibel, if she can play chess with him, but he tells her, 'girls do not play chess'. Beth has a flashback of her father leaving them as well as her mother's PhD thesis (object archetype).

In this example, the steps closely match the Hero's Journey:

ACT 1

- **Home World:** Elizabeth is sent to an orphanage for girls in the 1950s after her mother tries to kill them both
- **Status Quo:** Elizabeth learns the rules of the orphanage
- **Dark Clouds:** she's told to follow them, or no one will want to adopt you
- **Flaw Exposed:** Elizabeth gets addicted to the tranquillisers
- **Save the Cat:** Beth saves her mother's PhD thesis
- **Inciting Incident:** she watches Shaibel, the janitor, play chess and is intrigued
- **Antagonist:** Borgov, the Russian Grandmaster and Shaibel
- **Bad Behaviour:** takes the tranquilliser at night and visualises a chess board
- **Refusal:** she leaves the basement when Shaibel tells her he doesn't play strangers
- **Leave Home:** Shaibel tells her that girls don't play chess, but she changes his mind

ACT 2

- **Alien World:** Shaibel's basement
- **Mentor:** Jolene tells Beth not to get addicted to tranquillisers. Shaibel teaches her how to play chess
- **Friends and Enemies:** Jolene is also a friend. Beth plays against someone from the local Chess Club
- **Midpoint:** she beats Shaibel
- **Ultimate Test and Significant Death:** Beth is banned from playing chess with Shaibel and the school stops handing out tranquillisers (which she believes helps her at chess)

ACT 3

- **Shadow World:** Beth visits the local High School
- **All or Nothing:** she takes on the school's chess club in a simultaneous match
- **Suit Up:** Beth's in smart clothes
- **Final Fight:** she faces the male chess team
- **Out for the Count:** without her tranquillisers, she's miserable
- **Reborn:** Jolene gives Beth two tranquillisers
- **Special Move:** Beth takes the tranquillisers
- **Outcome:** Beth beats them all
- **Reward:** she's given a box of chocolates

There are some variations worth pointing out. Firstly, the Shadow World was relatively easy to enter – she was invited. And secondly, she was never quite **Out for the Count**. Miserable, yes; flat out, no. Also both Shaibel and Jolene don't fit neatly into either the mentor or friend character archetypes. Through the **flash forward**, Bogove is flagged as the ultimate antagonist, but to give Beth something to push against in episode 1, she has Shaibel. And although Jolene is like a school friend, she delivers the key piece of advice in the story about drugs (and will return later to remind her). Interestingly, the episode doesn't finish at the **Reward**. Beth, desperate for the tranquillisers, breaks into the pharmacy, and takes a mouthful of tranquillisers and passes out, falling to the floor. So here we have her entering a forbidden, dangerous world and being **Out for the Count**. In doing so, this converts the High School to an Alien World, and the pharmacy to the Shadow World.

A lot of what's just been said is semantics. What's key is not whether you include *every step* in the Hero's Journey, or have them in the *right order*, or make the mentor or friend archetypes clear cut, but how you use the tools the Hero's Journey provides to tell a great story.

INCITING INCIDENT AND THE FINAL FIGHT

As you've seen with the Symmetry Table earlier, it's common for scenes to have an opposite. One pair of the Hero's Journey steps have a particular connection too: the Inciting Incident and the Final Fight. These pairings exist in different combinations, which I've given names to:

1. Eager
2. Unconfident
3. Accidental
4. Foolhardy
5. Reckless
6. Cursed

I'll now explain each one with examples.

EAGER

If our protagonist is a **willing** hero, they've probably been duped into taking on an impossible task, and will seek retribution in Act 3. When they take on the quest, those encouraging them expect our hero to fail or never return. But when they miraculously survive and find out they were deceived, they'll want payback from those that tricked them. This pairing works well with war stories, where a naïve person may sign up believing it's the right thing to do. When they experience the horrors of war, they feel betrayed.

Born on the Fourth of July

This film is a biopic of Ron Kovic. He was a US soldier in the Vietnam War in which he was shot, paralysing him from the waist down. When Ron returns home, he becomes an anti-war activist. His transformation is emboldened by the poor rehabilitary support offered to veterans. His Home World effectively becomes the Shadow World.

UNCONFIDENT

If our protagonist begins as someone hesitant or unsure, they'll transform into someone brimming with confidence by the end. This format is standard fare in superhero stories or those about high school nerds who take on the bullies. It's a **zero-to-hero** story.

The Silence of the Lambs

Clarice Starling is a young, diminutive, FBI cadet from the sticks in an era of Ivy League male recruits. She's nervous and unsure of herself. Her boss asks her to interview a cannibalistic prisoner (Hannibal Lecter) to help them with a serial killer case. She agrees, but Hannibal manipulates her, and he escapes. Clarice grows in confidence and persuades him to help her track down the murderer.

ACCIDENTAL

In this scenario, our protagonist **stumbles** into the Alien World. When they do so, their focus will be on getting home ASAP. They'll not enjoy the strangeness of their new existence, and like Alice always be trying to get home. It's like taking a wrong turn when you're in a rush and find yourself lost. The *SAW* franchise uses this format.

The Wizard of Oz

Dorothy is whisked away by a tornado to a strange, frightening and technicolour land. From her arrival, Dorothy is desperate to get home. Sure, there are a moments of singalong fun, but she's relentless in her desire to return to Kansas.

FOOLHARDY

In this combination, our protagonist makes a rash decision and comes to regret it. By the end, they'll realise they've made a huge mistake and want their life to return to the way it was. This story combination works well in horror movies, when an overly curious protagonist unleashes an unholy curse. In *The Cabin in the Woods*, Dana reads from a book, awakening a family of zombies.

Toy Story

When Woody pushes Buzz out of the window due to jealousy, he spends the rest of the movie trying to correct his mistake. Near the end, Woody tells Buzz to leave him to the mercy of Sid as he's the inferior toy, but Buzz realises that they're both vital to Andy's life, and rescues him.

RECKLESS

In this pairing, our hero makes too quick a decision, and regrets what they've done. They think they've found an easy way out of a predicament or a shortcut to their goal. They persevere in the hope that others will bend to their will. But they pay the price for their overconfidence, often with tragic circumstances.

One Flew Over the Cuckoo's Nest

In this film, a criminal (probably with ADHD) pleads insanity to avoid labour duties. However, the easy life he thought he'd have in a mental institution is anything but. He's bored and riles the staff and other inmates for entertainment (or dopamine). Despite multiple warnings of what might happen, his rebellious behaviour escalates, and those in charge remove him. When he returns, he's been lobotomised.

CURSED

Someone transforms the protagonist using magic or subterfuge. This spell might be cast to teach someone a lesson or to have fun at someone else's expense. In *Trading Places*, two wealthy brothers swap the lives of two individuals – a street hustler and a commodities broker – for a bet. But the two guinea pigs turn the tables on them, wiping out their fortune.

Liar Liar

Fletcher Reede is an obnoxious, lying, divorced father who keeps letting down his son, Max. Max misses his father and **wishes** that his dad told the truth. It comes true and leads to humorous consequences as Fletcher attempts to lie, but finds he can't. Finally, through lots of misfortune, he learns the benign power of telling the truth.

Each pair feels like the right combination of cause-and-effect. Perhaps this is because the outcomes feel morally just. If you're too eager (1), perhaps you've not thought things through well enough, and you should pay for your rashness. Or if you begin your journey lacking confidence, through each hurdle jumped, you'll grow more confident (2). Or for 3, if you're so careless as to end up in the wrong place, you'll regret it, and want to return home as quickly as possible.

SIGNIFICANT DEATH AND PSEUDO DEATH

The Significant Death is a key step in the Hero's Journey. It occurs around the two-thirds point of a story. Whether it's Grandpa in *Little Miss Sunshine* or Chico in *Dirty Harry*, it's a shocking and sad event. (Even though Harry's junior partner, Chico, survives being shot, he quits – death by another name).

The Significant Death forces our protagonist to go it alone and raises the difficulty of achieving their ultimate goal. So common is the Significant Death in stories that when it doesn't happen, or occurs at a different point, it's a shock. When Julia Montague, one of the main characters in *Bodyguard*, is killed in the middle of the series, it created quite a furore. With Julia's body not shown, many viewers thought her death was faked. But by placing her death at the Midpoint it fulfilled David's 180-degree transformation. He was Julia's Specialist Protection Officer, tasked with keeping her safe. By failing to do this, he's the opposite of what he was.

This subversion of expectations demonstrates the flexibility of the Hero's Journey again or stories more generally. But there's a consequence if you move the Significant Death to the Midpoint: the **Pseudo Death**. The Pseudo Death is not an actual death but something close to it that occurs at the now vacant point the Significant Death would normally occur.

In *Bodyguard*, David shoots himself and collapses. It appears that he's killed himself. But the bullets have been replaced by blanks (unbeknownst to him), and he survives. So it looked like he died but he didn't. Let's look at two more examples:

1917

Two British soldiers are tasked to deliver a message deep into German-held territory. At the Midpoint, Lance Corporal Blake is killed by a downed German pilot. Schofield is left alone to complete the mission. At the three-quarters mark, Lance Corporal Schofield gets shot by a German soldier in the head — the screen goes black. But he gets up, saved by his helmet.

Star Wars: Episode VIII — The Last Jedi

Luke Skywalker reluctantly trains Rey in the Force. At the Midpoint, Kylo brings Rey to Snoke, as instructed. But when Snoke tries to force Kylo to kill her, he unexpectedly kills Snoke. Later, with the First Order about to overcome the Resistance stronghold, Luke sacrifices himself to buy them time and becomes one with the Force (semi-dead).

06.

THE
HEART
PLOT

Previously, I've described the Mind Plot — the external journey our protagonist takes to get what they want. The Heart Plot documents their emotional journey. It describes how they feel about events and how it changes them. The Heart Plot is synergistic with the Mind Plot, i.e., each action has a reaction — an impact on their emotional status. And as they are transformed internally, this impacts how they behave.

The Heart Plot should be a melodic rollercoaster: 'Melodies, like sentences, often have halfway stopping places, the equivalent of commas, semicolons, and colons in writing' (*What to Listen for in Music*). The more combinations of 'external event > internal change' you can create, the more detailed and believable their transformation will be.

Vogler and Yorke both pioneered this approach. I'll describe the transitions in sets of three, one for each Act. I've split Act 2 into 2A, 2B, and 2C. If you look at Table 9 you'll see how this split works in terms of approximate script percentage and beats.

ACT 1	ACT 2A	ACT 2B	ACT 2C	ACT 3
20%	*22%*	*22%*	*22%*	*15%*
9-10 beats	10-11 beats	10-11 beats	10-11 beats	11-17 beats

Table 9: Act Structure.

ACT 1

Unaware ⟶ **Some awareness** ⟶ **Completely aware**

In Act 1, our protagonist is entirely unaware of any impending danger. As the Act progresses, they become increasingly conscious that something is wrong in their world or their life. Following the Inciting Incident, they can't ignore things any longer, and a correction is needed, they exit their Home World and enter an Alien one.

Another Round

This film is about four friends (three are teachers) who turn to alcohol to solve their problems. The teachers' students are uninspired and disappointed with them; Nikolaj isn't being a good father. The protagonist, Martin, is told by his wife that he's no longer the man she married. Martin agrees to do better for his wife and his students.

Knives Out

Marta is a private nurse (and friend) of Harlan Thrombey, a patriarch of a successful, family business. When he dies, she returns to his mansion, where most of the family have gathered. With each interaction, Marta realises that they don't cherish her the way Harlan did. Blanc, the detective, believes his death was murder.

ACT 2A

Resistant ⟶ Hesitant ⟶ Give it a go

In Act 2A, the Inciting Incident has launched our protagonist into an Alien World. It's a shock, and they struggle to cope. But with the help of a mentor or friends, they acclimatise. They learn through listening, watching, and doing.

Another Round

Martin's not keen on drinking, even at a celebratory meal. He also refuses to dance. Nikolaj tells them of a theory that humans were designed to always have a small percentage of alcohol in their bloodstream. The benefits from doing so appear to offer them solutions to their problems. They start drinking every day.

Knives Out

Marta cannot lie without puking, but she'll need to lie to hide her accidental involvement in Harlan's death. Harlan (the Mentor) teaches her to lie through omission. Despite her reservations, she uses the technique with Blanc, and avoids throwing up when questioned.

ACT 2B

New skills/ knowledge ⟶ **Midpoint** ⟶ **New skills/ knowledge**

In Act 2B, we cover events either side of the Midpoint. Pre-Midpoint, our protagonist, is closer to the person at the beginning than after the Midpoint, when they're closer to their final form. This progression is achieved through the acquisition of new skills and knowledge.

Another Round

Martin becomes more authoritative and expressive in the classroom. The others see improvements in their life too. After the Midpoint, the teachers have transformed from poor to good teachers, and become more fun generally.

Knives Out

Marta continues to cover up her involvement in Harlan's death. At the Midpoint, Ransom arrives. The will reading reveals that Harlan has left his estate to Marta. His family are outraged, so she escapes with Ransom, the black sheep. She confesses her involvement in Harlan's death, and he offers to help her keep the money, if she cuts him in on it.

ACT 2C

Question ⟶ **Regret** ⟶ **Crisis**

In Act 2C, our protagonist suffers an existential meltdown. With their new persona, they utilise their acquired skills but question who they've become. They feel remorse then reach a crisis point at the end of Act 2.

Another Round

Nikolaj proposes drinking even more. Martin questions this escalation while the other two support it. Finally, Martin relents, and they go on a bender. Martin passes out drunk in the street. His wife tells him she's seeing someone else. Martin walks out. The four friends agree that the experiment's gone too far and decide to stop.

Knives Out

Marta tells her mother she doesn't like the associated attention due to being left the inheritance. Harlan's family threaten to expose her mother's (possible) illegal entry into the country. Marta receives a letter that states the sender knows the part she played in Harlan's death, and they've got evidence. In desperation, Marta goes to Ransom for help.

ACT 3

Rejuvenated ⟶ Demonstrate ⟶ Enlightened

In the final Act, our protagonist begins at a low point after the Significant Death. Their efforts so far to reach their goal have failed. When all appears lost, they enter the Shadow World for one final attempt. Since their previous methods have been unsuccessful, they finally address their flaw and try something different.

Another Round

The teachers return to school. Martin and Peter are sober, but Tommy arrives drunk – he's become an alcoholic. Martin meets his wife and apologises for his behaviour. He should've told her something was wrong. Peter learns that a small drink in the right circumstances can be helpful. Martin's and Peter's students pass. Tommy dies. Martin drinks to celebrate their achievements and dances, finding the joy in life he was missing.

Knives Out

Marta believes that if she can destroy the remaining copy of the incriminating evidence, she'll be in the clear. She drives into town with Ransom to meet the blackmailer, but Blanc arrests them. Marta tricks Blanc and goes to meet the blackmailer alone and finds Fran, the housekeeper, unconscious. When Blanc confronts Marta and Ransom at the house, instead of lying to protect herself, she lies to trick Ransom into confessing. She realises what Harlan knew all along, that she deserved the wealth more than them.

07.

EXCEPTIONS

It should go without saying that there are exceptions to every supposed rule. But if you don't know the rules, how do you know if you're breaking them? You've seen how flexible the Hero's Journey is as a template and that it's only one of several. Andrei Tarkovsky was a Russian filmmaker whose films barely follow the Hero's Journey yet they're gripping, with evolving characters and shocking events. The modern equivalent is Christopher Nolan, whose films have clever premises and complex plots that are also highly entertaining.

CHAOS STORIES

A Chaos Story is one where the protagonist undergoes little emotional change and is dominated by the plot. They're usually action films. Best suited to the big screen, they're full of fights, explosions, and exotic locations. Examples include *The Fast and the Furious*, *James Bond*, *John Wick*, *Atomic Blonde*, and *Bullet Train*. These films prioritise plot over character.

This isn't to say there aren't distinctive protagonists but that they become the equivalent of a lone croûton tossed endlessly in a salad. They tumble from one crisis to another in more and more ridiculous ways. Without much of a Heart Plot, the Mind Plot dominates, with each explosive event driving the story forwards, with little impact on the protagonist's emotional state. Twists and reversals add complexity.

A classic example is *The Invisible Man*, written by H G Wells. A scientist called Griffin renders himself invisible. He tries to reverse the procedure while trying to keep his affliction secret. It's a breathless read. Griffin spends most of the story running from place to place to escape detection, while trying to find a chemical solution. He becomes increasingly desperate, killing when cornered, and is eventually beaten to death by an angry mob.

These Chaos Stories, with plenty of action and little internal growth in the protagonist, have strong commercial potential. They don't all need to be action heroes. Forrest is a disabled man with learning difficulties who influences others, often through happenstance (*Forrest Gump*). Chaos Stories are mostly Act 2. *Waiting for Godot* is another example. You're straight into the action with no clear explanation of what will happen to them when Godot arrives. And although there are no explosions or location changes in the play, it's so entertaining it holds our attention.

A recent film with elements of a Chaos Story is *Everything Everywhere All at Once*. Whether that's in part due to one of the writer's having ADHD is something to consider. This film manages to achieve a feeling of chaotic excitement while also developing the main characters' relationships with each other.

COINCIDENCE

Coincidences happen in life, but they shouldn't happen in stories. Or at least not often – once is okay. If the protagonist reaches their goal through luck, it will feel unearned. It can work if a coincidental meeting is revealed as a plot twist later. In *The Worst Person in the World*, Julie gatecrashes a party and spends the rest of the evening with a man she meets. They desperately try to avoid intimacy so as not to cheat on their partners.

Although stories should avoid coincidences, chance encounters can be exciting. *Brief Encounter* tells a non-idealised tale about a couple unhappy in their respective marriages. *Lost in Translation* is about two lonely strangers who spend an evening together after meeting in a Tokyo bar. In *Palm Springs*, two people live the same day again and again. In *Compartment Number 6*, conflict arises from the incompatibility of two travellers stuck together in a train carriage.

In each of these films, the unexpected meeting of two characters, usually worlds apart, starts an adventure.

MOMENT OF WONDER

A Moment of Wonder (MOW) is a surprising and arresting visual event. They usually have no major impact on a plot. Time seems to stop. Some examples:

- Martin's dance at the end of *Another Round*
- Grant lays eyes on a living, breathing, Brontosaurus in *Jurassic Park*
- Niles and Sarah watch dinosaurs stroll past in *Palm Springs*
- In *Nope*, the alien creature fully extends itself in the sky
- Ellie watches the escaped giraffes stride in *The Last of Us*
- The Sirens in *O Brother, Where Are Thou?*
- In *Aliens*, when Ripley emerges from the lift in a Powered Work Loader
- When the truck bursts through the barrier in *Terminator 2: Judgment Day*
- In *Butch Cassidy and the Sundance Kid*, when they jump off the cliff
- Alexia tries to trigger a miscarriage in *Titane*
- *Independence Day*, when the alien mothership vaporises the White House
- In *Magnolia*, it rains frogs

MOWs can be disturbing e.g. when Lydia Tár hears screaming in the forest (*Tár*). It's a break in the action, reminds us of our protagonist's situation and is a hiatus from their journey's relentless forward momentum.

A MOW bears some resemblance to a **bottle episode**. A bottle episode does not relate to the main episode and it may not even feature the protagonist. For example, 'Beard After Hours', in the series *Ted Lasso* is set mainly outside the football stadium and focuses on one of the quieter secondary characters. MOWs give the writer or director the chance to add an artistic flourish.

GENRE

Genre affects the story's tone through expected tropes unique to each one. If the Hero's Journey is the frame of a building, genre is the architectural style e.g. Art Deco or Georgian. Some say every movie is a genre movie. Rather than get too academic, let's see how genre can help us write a story. I'll use the Western, one of the most enduring and flexible, to do this.

WESTERN

The Western genre originates from America's Wild West, where frontier life provided a rich source of characters and events to create stories. The Western has moved through periods of historical accuracy, romanticism, reflection, and reinvention periods. This era was a time of adventure and risk, where families colonised vast swathes of countryside, populated by native Americans or Mexicans. This ingress often led to conflict, as depicted in early Western films such as *The Big Trail*, *The Great K & A Train Robbery*, or *The Alamo*.

As towns were established, the rule of law was enforced by the Sheriff. This leant itself to the evergreen trope of cops and robbers – often in the form of a solitary lawman (or similar) holding out against a group of outlaws e.g. *Tombstone*, *3:10 to Yuma*. *Dances with Wolves*, released in 1990, was a romantic take on the genre, whereas *Unforgiven*, released two years later, is more critical of the period. Regardless of the type of Western, several tropes appear again and again:

Exceptions.

- Isolated towns
- Railroad
- Outlaws
- Landowners
- Barren landscapes
- Horses and cattle
- The saloon
- The Marshall or Sheriff

The Western genre is also a staple of TV from *The Life and Legend of Wyatt Earp* to *Yellowstone*. *Banshee* is a town where a thief pretends to be the new Sheriff. *Justified* follows a U.S. Marshal sent back to his hometown in eastern Kentucky. *Hap and Leonard* is set in the 1980s and follows two friends – a white peace activist and a black ex-vet. The maverick cop trope, e.g. *Dirty Harry*, *Judge Dredd*, *Lethal Weapon*, is a throwback to Westerns, when Marshalls and Sheriffs had to make on-the-spot judgements. And like many heavily used genres, they become ripe for parody e.g. *Blazing Saddles*, *Sledge Hammer*.

The Western genre's universal themes e.g. law and order and exploration make it malleable into other stories. One of the best examples is *The Magnificent Seven*. This Hollywood epic, full of stars, was a remake of the Japanese film, *Seven Samurai* (based on *The Water Margin*). Both films tell the story of seven outlaws who band together to protect a defenceless village. But thematically there was also a remarkable overlap. At that time in Japan's history, central government was phasing out the samurai just as the hired guns in *The Magnificent Seven* knew their time was also coming to an end.

A good way to create a fresh premise, is to mix two genres. The Western has proved good for hybridisation. Here are some examples:

- **Comedy x Western:** *Blazing Saddles, City Slickers*
- **Sci-Fi x Western:** *Total Recall, Firefly, Blakes Seven*
- **Horror x Western:** *The Walking Dead, Stan meets Evil, Nope*
- **Fantasy x Western:** *Star Wars, The Dark Tower*

In the *Star Wars* universe, the Jedi are similar to the hired gun or the samurai. Swords become light sabres. And any saloon has elements of a Western one — grizzly drinkers, odd music, and games of chance, all under the watchful eye of a female owner.

NON-LINEAR NARRATIVES

Non-linear narratives are stories where the events are told out of sequence. They can take multiple forms and while **flashbacks** and **flashforwards** are their bread and butter, more complex methods exist. For example, you can have whole Acts told out of sequence, such as *Memento*, where one story is told forward, while another runs backwards. Flashbacks and flashforwards:

- Provide intrigue by giving a glimpse of something before or after the current action that's unexpected
- Flashbacks reveal backstories that explain a character's behaviour or recent events
- Flashforwards give a glimpse of a future that seems unlikely, given current circumstances

Uncharted begins with Nathan Drake tumbling across cargo flowing out of the back of a transport plane (flashforward). We then switch back in time to him as a child (flashback) before jumping forward to the present day. In three scenes, we see the after, before, and the present. It's a concise reveal of some of Nathan's backstory as well as having the benefit of a big action scene to kick off the film.

When it comes to a movie like *Pulp Fiction*; it's hard to imagine it in any other way than being non-linear. They say that a film's made in three stages: the writing, the filming, and the editing. If *Pulp Fiction*'s non-linear narrative was created in the edit, the Hero's Journey might explain why it works so well.

Pulp Fiction

Pulp Fiction has three interweaving stories that don't run in a chronological sequence. It also has three protagonists: Jules, Vincent and Butch, and one antagonist, Marsellus. Of our three heroes, Jules changes the most, Butch, somewhat, and Vincent not at all. Jules begins as an atheist, is a believer at the Midpoint, and seeks redemption at the end. Jules is not in all the scenes, so the protagonist's role in the Hero's Journey is shared. To demonstrate this, I've reordered Pulp Fiction into a Hero's Journey.

PROLOGUE

Honey and Pumpkin are in a restaurant discussing whether they will do **something** again. They eventually agree to rob the restaurant rather than a bank, as this should make it less likely that someone will play at being a hero.

ACT 1

- **Protagonist:** Jules, smartly dressed, drives a nice car. His colleague Vincent sits in the passenger seat
- **Home World:** the rougher side of Hollywood
- **Status Quo:** Jules and Vincent are killers who visit Brett and his friends to collect an item belonging to their boss, Marsellus Wallace
- **Dark Clouds:** Jules quotes from the Bible. His lifestyle's based on his interpretation that he's righteous in taking vengeance on those that cross their boss (his God). But the passage also states that God truly blesses those who help those that have done wrong
- **Mentor:** God, via the Bible passage
- **Flaw Exposed:** Jules is insular and inflexible. He needs to be more curious and considerate
- **Save the Cat:** Jules shoots Brett's colleague in the shoulder rather than killing him

- **Antagonist:** Vincent and Jules visit Marsellus
- **Inciting Incident:** Marsellus asks Vincent to take his wife, Mia, out for dinner
- **Want:** Vincent wants to do what his boss tells him to
- **Bad Behaviour:** Vincent agrees, despite Jules's warnings
- **Friends:** Vincent buys a bag of heroin for himself from his drug dealer, Lance
- **Take Off:** Vincent picks up the coke-addicted Mia and takes her to dinner

ACT 2

- **Alien World:** a 1950s-themed restaurant
- **Obstacles:** Vincent and Mia dance together
- **Another Alien World:** Marsellus's posh house
- **Obstacles:** Mia takes the heroin thinking it's coke and overdoses. Vincent takes her to Lance's and saves her with an adrenaline shot to the heart
- **Midpoint:** Butch doesn't throw a fight as he agreed to do for Marsellus. His opponent dies
- **Ultimate Test:** Butch returns to his flat to collect his father's watch, despite knowing Marsellus may have men nearby
- **Significant Death:** Butch kills Vincent

ACT 3

- **Shadow World:** Pawn shop basement. Marsellus and Butch are tied up
- **All or Nothing:** Butch escapes
- **Suit Up:** Butch grabs a samurai sword
- **Final Fight:** Butch returns to save Marsellus:
    1. **Out for the Count:** Butch knocks out the Gimp
    2. **Reborn:** Butch kills Maynard with the sword
    3. **Special Move:** Marsellus shoots Zed
    4. **Success:** they escape

At this point, the film could end but it doesn't.

EPILOGUE

We're in the past, when Vincent is still alive, back with Brett and his friends. A man appears and shoots at them but all the bullets miss. They kill him and take Marvin in the car. Vincent accidentally kills Marvin. Wolf, a fixer, arrives to help them destroy the evidence. Vincent and Jules go to the restaurant (from the first scene), where Jules states he's retiring.

Vincent goes to the restroom. Honey and Pumpkin start their rampage. When they reach Jules, they want the suitcase, but he refuses to give it to them. He has a gun pointed at them under the table. He lets them live and his transformation is complete: an instrument of vengeance to a calm shepherd, ready to wander the earth.

Let's look at the Heart Plot now so we can appreciate Jules's internal transformation:

HEART PLOT

Jules's conversion is dramatic. He goes from someone who'd shoot first and ask questions later, to someone who uses diplomacy to de-escalate a dangerous situation.

Unaware ⟶ **Some awareness** ⟶ **Completely aware**

Jules knows little about the outside world. He's intrigued by Vincent's stories of another culture. He's unaware of the intimacy associated with a foot massage, but he's certain that taking out their boss's wife for the evening is a bad idea.

Resistant ⟶ Hesitant ⟶ Give it a go

Jules is polite to the three men who have Marsellus's suitcase. He uses his new knowledge of hamburgers to strike up a conversation. When one of the men doesn't follow his orders, Jules shoots him in the shoulder, rather than in the head.

**New skills/ ⟶ Midpoint ⟶ New skills/
knowledge   knowledge**

Jules learns that even when you think you're safe, you're not. They survive being shot at. Jules believes this was a divine intervention (Vincent doesn't).

Question ⟶ Regret ⟶ Crisis

Jules questions what just happened. He decides to retire and will tell Marsellus when they give him the suitcase. Vincent accidentally shoots Marvin, covering them and the car in blood.

Rejuvenated ⟶ Demonstrate ⟶ Enlightened

Jules (with help) cleans up the mess. He washes and gets new clothes (**Suit Up**). In the diner, Jules refuses to eat pork. When confronted by Pumpkin and Honey, rather than shoot them, he talks them down. He leaves the restaurant with Vincent to hand in his notice.

08.

CHARACTER

People often say that character and plot are immiscible, that you can't have one without the other. But when I think about the most memorable characters, what they do is secondary. You know them so well, you could predict how they'd behave in any circumstance, not just the ones they're known for. This section is about how to create memorable characters.

Many of the best-known characters are from sitcoms or long-running series, where they're **larger than life**. For example Kramer or George (*Seinfeld*), Leslie Knope or Ron Swanson (*Parks and Recreation*), Walter White or Saul Goodman (*Breaking Bad*, *Better Call Saul*), Tony (*The Sopranos*), Del Boy, Rodney and Trigger (*Only Fools and Horses*).

These remarkable characters dominate every scene they're in and warp the world to their will. It seems improbable they could live in the real world. But perhaps you do know an eccentric character in real life that could inspire you. Or have you read about a historical figure that's intriguing? Once you have the outline of a character, here are some ways to flesh them out.

MONOLOGUES

Record a spoken monologue or write one, embodying your character. You could pretend your figure is on Speakers Corner in London, telling everyone how the world should be. If it's the villain, it might explain the motivation for their dastardly plan. Or you might imagine the character in a private moment, e.g. talking to their child at their bedside. Perhaps they reveal a secret. In *Better Call Saul*, Gus Fring tells a story at the bedside of an unconscious Hector Salamanca, his nemesis. It's a childhood story of how he captured a wild animal that had eaten the fruit from a tree he'd grown from a seedling. His vengeance on the animal paralleled what he'd done to Hector. Another option is to write the monologues as diary entries. What would your character say when no one else is listening?

QUESTIONS

A popular method to create fuller characters is to ask them questions and jot down their answers. Here are some you could use:

- What's your favourite
  - Colour?
  - Film?
  - Food?
  - Hobbies?
  - Season?
  - Drink?
  - Toy?
  - Song?
- Where do you live?
- What did you have for breakfast?
- When were you most embarrassed?
- When were you at your loneliest?
- What stops you from achieving your goals?
- When are you most relaxed?
- Have you ever been violent?
- If you had three wishes, what would they be?
- Are you happy with your life?
- When were you at your happiest?
- When were you at your lowest?
- What's the best thing you've ever done?
- What's the worst thing you've ever done to yourself?
- What's the worst thing you've ever done to another person?
- What's the worst thing that anyone has done to you?
- What's your biggest secret?
- What kind of person do you present yourself as in public?
- What do you hide from other people?
- What do you like about your physical appearance?

- What would you change about your physical appearance?
- Who do you love?
    - What's the worst thing you can imagine happening to them?
    - What would be the best way of hurting that person?
- Have you ever broken someone's heart, and if so, who?
- What was the last dream you had?
    - What do you think the dream meant if anything?
- Where would you like to travel to?
- When did you last laugh, and what made it happen?
- When did you last cry, and what made that happen?
- What was the last joke you told, and did anyone laugh?
- What keeps you awake at night?
- What are you most afraid of?
- What do you believe happens after you die?
- Who do you hate?
- What do people say about you behind your back?
- What do you think your family say about you behind your back?
- What do you contribute to the world?
- What would you change about the world?
- List three things that make life worth living
- Write down your worst flaw
- What do you want?
- What do you need?
- What's in your pocket?

MEMORIES

Another technique for developing a character is to write down things they remember. The key to this method's success relies on a phenomenon experienced with **free writing**. Free writing is to write without a prompt but usually for a set period of time. At a certain point, when you've run out of all the mundane, obvious things to write, such as what you ate for lunch, the surroundings etc., something unexpected happens. It's as if your conscious mind hands over control to your subconscious. Memories appear that have no connection to your lived experience. A way to encourage this switchover is to use a timer and to give yourself an ambitious target of memories to recall. For example, 10 minutes for 50 recollections. You're allowed to write a single word, up to a sentence, for each one. It's unlikely you'll hit 50, but the pressure of trying to reach that number should generate some unexpected memories.

THE PROTAGONIST

The protagonist is the central character of our story and experiences most, if not all, of the events within the Mind and Heart Plots. Whether they're heroic or not, they're the hero in the Hero's Journey. There might be more than one, e.g. *Pulp Fiction*, *Thelma and Louise*, *Cagney and Lacey*, but they all can benefit from having some of the following characteristics:

1. Interesting
2. Selfless
3. Relatable
4. Want and Need
5. Superpower
6. Flawed
7. Active
8. Fallible
9. Resilient
10. Malleable

Let's go through each one.

INTERESTING

Your protagonist should be interesting. If they are, the audience will want to watch them. They'll want to see how they tackle different obstacles and follow them through the story. Your protagonist doesn't have to be attractive, or likeable, to be interesting. Although historically, this was often the case. Hitchcock chose good-looking leads. Unless it's essential to your story, don't specify it in your writing.

Being overly specific about the physical characteristics of your protagonist can be problematic. After all, you want the broadest range of readers to empathise with your protagonist and the best actors to want to play them. A surefire way to make your protagonist interesting is if they say or do exciting things. And if you must choose between the two, make it what they do.

If a protagonist does interesting things, they can get away with being somewhat bland. In franchises such as James Bond or John Wick, it's their profession and their unique skills that hold our interest. In these types of films, the other characters, particularly the 'baddies', are usually far more interesting e.g. Odd Job, Jaws, or Poe in *Altered Carbon*.

The action figure leads hold our attention because of the fantastical things they do (and the quips they throw). The danger comes in the down moments, when they're not being superheroic. The solution to this is to make their ordinary life just as tricky e.g. Buffy, Superman and Lois. The protagonist should be as intriguing as you can make them.

SELFLESS

If we empathise with the protagonist, we'll feel connected to them and want to keep watching. The way to achieve this is to make them do something selfless. Blake Snyder called this the *Save the Cat* moment. Our hero should do something helpful for someone or something else with no personal gain.

Ironically, the use of cats has become something of an in-joke with cats regularly used, e.g. *Russian Doll, Uncharted*. Other animals work too, e.g. migrating geese in *The Sopranos*, a neighbour's dog (*Mr Robot*) or an upside-down cockroach in *Three Billboards Outside Ebbing, Missouri*.

In shows where the lead's profession is, by its nature, caring, they'll go over and beyond what would be expected of the role, e.g. Superman picking up a kid's cap after catching a falling car (*Superman and Lois*). Not all protagonists should have a selfless moment. For some, e.g. Batman, it's skippable. You know that he is relentless in his prioritisation of others over himself. For some, they can't take the risk. In Obi-Wan Kenobi, Ben is hiding from the First Order. If he demonstrates selfless behaviour, that will expose him. When he has an opportunity to help a co-worker, he doesn't. However, we do see him smuggling a chunk of meat for his camel-like transport, but this action isn't selfless. After all, if he doesn't feed it, it will die, and he'll have no way to get to and from home. But this is an illicit treat telling us that Ben's caring nature is still present.

You may also skip this moment in a playful way – almost daring the audience not to like the protagonist. In the opening scene of *Killing Eve*, Villanelle is upset that she can't make a child smile, so as she leaves she knocks the girl's ice cream into her lap. This **Kick the Puppy** type behaviour is ideally suited for your antagonist.

RELATABLE

A protagonist should be relatable. It's hard to invest in a character that's too different from us because if they are, how could their journey teach us anything? At the basic level of human existence, we all need the same things: food, safety, sleep etc. Showing your protagonist being ordinary can make them relatable. Eating breakfast or being bored at work can work. Just don't overdo it.

Make the action specific e.g. Ruben makes a (loud) smoothie (*Sound of Metal*) or Truman Burbank being super excited for work (*The Truman Show*). Superheroes are rarely relatable, but they can be aspirational. They provide a saviour character for us (like Jesus). If they do something we do, we'll relate to them more but it may take some of the gloss off their character, so use with caution.

WANT AND NEED

Your protagonist should have two drivers: an external **want** and an internal **need**. Wants and needs are often confused with each other. A **want** is something that is over and above our basic needs. It may seem superficial, but it's an overriding goal that pushes them forward. It could be a desire for friendship, love, or career success.

In *Sound of Metal*, Ruben wants to be in a band with his girlfriend. In *Jaws*, Brody wants to protect the town. It may appear intense or obsessive. When it's disrupted, or an opportunity emerges, they do all they can to protect or get it.

Hidden away is our protagonist's **need**. This is an internal desire that they've buried. Ruben needs to find inner peace (and let his girlfriend leave the band). Brody must overcome his fear of water (to kill the shark). Whether your protagonist gets either their want or need is up to you.

It can help to summarise what your character wants and needs in a sentence. For example, in *Star Wars: Episode IV: A New Hope*, Luke wants adventure but needs family. In *Chinatown*, Gettes intends to solve the mystery of the missing woman but needs to not to repeat the mistakes of the past.

Your protagonist's want is fulfilled by the Mind Plot and the need by the Heart Plot. The Mind Plot dominates many stories, such as action, thrillers, detective, or sitcoms. The focus is on what happens externally with less attention given to our protagonist's inner self.

By the end of your story, four combinations of outcomes are possible:

1. The protagonist gets what they want **and** what they need
2. The protagonist gets what they want but **not** what they need
3. The protagonist **doesn't** get what they want but **does** get what they need
4. The protagonist **doesn't** get what they want **or** what they need

In *Chinatown*, Gettes finds the missing woman but fails to protect her. In *Star Wars: Episode IV: A New Hope*, Skywalker finds adventure but loses his foster parents. (In subsequent films he finds friends, a sister, and discovers his father is alive).

SUPERPOWER

You've now built a protagonist with some complexity. What they could do with now is a **superpower**. This attribute is something they're better at than anyone else in our story (with the possible exception of the antagonist or mentor). The superpower doesn't need to be objectively positive but from their perspective, they're good at it. It's easiest to see in comic book characters as they are often an exaggeration of athletic prowess, e.g. running, jumping, swimming, boxing. However, in most stories, you're not writing about superheroes, so your protagonist's superpower needs to be more down-to-earth.

In the play, *The Girl Who Was Very Good at Lying*, Catriona is great at making up stories. It may be morally dubious but makes for a fun superpower. Saul Goodman is great at scamming (*Better Call Saul, Breaking Bad*) and Walter White is adept at chemistry. Beth is gifted at chess (*The Queen's Gambit*). In *Bodyguard*, David's superpower is his quickness of thought. In the first episode, not only does he save his kids and the train passengers, but also the suicide bomber.

A superpower gives our hero something to help solve obstacles on their journey. We like to watch people who are good at something, if judged by the number of cooking, painting, dancing, and singing shows on TV. Sometimes the superpower is innate, but sometimes it's learnt, e.g. *The Karate Kid*, *Kingsman: The Secret Service*. When a superpower is used for misuse, it's often inherent, and when it's used for good, it's usually learnt. Whatever you choose, make it unique.

FLAWED

As well as seeing your protagonist excel, we need to see them falter due to their flaw. This weakness can be heroic, tragic, or comic, depending on the genre. In *Little Miss Sunshine*, Olive's final dance heads for disaster, but it's avoided when her father, the protagonist, corrects his flaw and jumps on stage. His belief that success is everything is shattered at this moment, when he realises by watching Olive, that it isn't. Her love for dancing is more important than whether she's any good at it.

Unless the protagonist is a superhero (Superman and kryptonite or David and water in *Unbreakable*) the hero's flaw is often subtle. Unless it's comedy, when the flaw is obvious and often, somewhat ridiculous. In *The Office*, David Brent believes that being popular is the key to being a good boss. In *Superstore*, Jonah's rebellious streak is ill-suited to working in a retail store. In sitcoms or long-running series they may never correct their flaw.

A typical human has many flaws. Character flaws in stories remind us that no one's perfect. In *Happy Valley*, when Sergeant Catherine Cawood attempts to prevent someone from setting fire to themselves, she exclaims, '... I'm divorced, I live with my sister... I've two grown-up children, one dead and one who doesn't speak to me.' These imperfections may hinder the protagonist but can also inspire them to do better.

In stories, our protagonist should have one major psychological flaw that holds them back. A mental or physical disability can give them obstacles to overcome but shouldn't be their flaw. In *Jerk*, the humour arises because Tim is unpleasant rather than because he has cerebral palsy.

The flaw should be related to their inner need, the thing that's stopping them from achieving enlightenment or true happiness. In *Bodyguard*, David has post-traumatic stress disorder. His unwillingness to seek help means it continually trips him up. The protagonist's flaw counterbalances their superpower, making them fallible. If they have no weakness, they don't have to take any risks, and the results of any conflict are inevitable. A flaw makes them human.

ACTIVE

Your intriguing, generous, human-like, talented, imperfect protagonist is now ready to go out into the world to chase their dream, unaware of what they need to be happy. They must lead the action, so make them do stuff. In most stories, this means going on a physical journey. *Thelma and Louise* go on a road trip, Stalker takes two men to the Zone (*Stalker*), Dorothy lands in Oz, and Neo enters the Matrix. When our hero chooses to enter the Alien World, we go with them.

In the Alien World, our protagonist learns the rules of their new environment. They actively listen to their mentor or friends around them. But it can't be too long before they retake the lead e.g. when Neo makes them go back for Morpheus. When your protagonist leads the action, barriers will rise. How they respond will determine how we see them. Their flaw should affect their actions which will have consequences for their progress toward their goal (Mind Plot). And each outcome will affect how they feel (Heart Plot).

If your protagonist doesn't take decisive action, the audience can lose interest e.g. in *Rogue One: A Star Wars Story*, Jyn Erso sometimes felt like a passenger. If they are truly learning and adapting, they should apply their new knowledge and skills to their quest.

Oddly, being active doesn't mean our protagonist is essential. In *Raiders of the Lost Ark*, if the actions of Indiana are removed, the Nazis still lose. Almost no one notices this, and it doesn't seem to diminish our enjoyment even when you realise it. We value his strong work ethic even if his actions are ultimately futile, like Sisyphus. Indiana makes decisions from the start and keeps making them. Whether he changes as a person matters less to us than if he wins. He's somewhat like James Bond or John Wick; you don't need them to overcome a flaw or reach self-enlightenment; we just need them to save the world.

FALLIBLE

Mistakes are learning opportunities. If our hero is fallible, they should make plenty. In real life, we tend to repeat the same mistakes again and again. But our protagonist isn't us; they should learn from them, and change their behaviour (in most cases). Their mistakes should primarily come from their flawed thinking.

David Brent's (*The Office*) unwavering belief in being popular rather than competent, prevents him from u-turning from a wrong decision. Instead, he often makes it worse by doubling down. Spiderman's overconfidence repeatedly gets him in trouble.

Because your protagonist leads the action, they must make decisions continually. And each one can't be right – that would be unbelievable, even if they weren't imperfect. Real life is more unpredictable.

When our protagonist is in the Alien World, they make mistakes through inexperience and naivety, as well as because of their flaw. As the story progresses, overconfidence in their new skills can cause them to fail. For example, when the detective accuses the wrong person of being the killer. In *See How They Run*, they use this as a running gag, with Constable Stalker repeatedly jumping to the wrong conclusion.

Clark often makes the wrong parenting choice in *Superman and Lois*. In *Rain Man*, Charlie Babbitt kidnaps his brother Raymond from an institution and then struggles to care for him.

(A neat symmetrical reversal of Raymond's mistake when they were children). Showing that our protagonist is fallible makes them human.

RESILIENT

Our protagonist should show resilience. If they give up, the story ends, after all. If they're active and making flawed decisions, mistakes will happen, and that should affect their progress and their emotional well-being. And your protagonist should always be there at the end, whether they succeed or fail.

So even if they lose a limb (Luke Skywalker, Ezra in *Prospect*) or an eye (Nick Fury, *Thor*), they must keep going. By the end of *Die Hard*, John McClane is so battered and bruised you can't believe he's still standing. But he reaches the top of the Nakatomi Plaza's tower to defeat Hans Gruber.

Demonstrating a *never-say-die* attitude, our protagonist shows us that no goal is unachievable. When our protagonist is flat out on the canvas, defeated, but somehow, they get up, we feel euphoric. And even if their victory is bittersweet e.g. *Butch Cassidy and the Sundance Kid*, *Thelma and Louise* or *Most Promising Young Woman*, they make it to the end credits (even if as a text message).

MALLEABLE

Our protagonist must be malleable so they can change. The protagonist's transformation from one persona to another is a vital story element. They must be a different person at the story's end. There are exceptions: the action hero, sitcom star, or the detective, but their inflexibility is unique to their genre. The rigidity of some characters can be part of their charm, e.g. Inspector Stoppard is unlikely to stop going to the pub (*See*

How They Run); Batman rarely holds back his punches; Captain Manwaring never listens to Sgt. Wilson, just as Sherlock Holmes ignores Lestrade and Watson.

For every other type of protagonist, though, we need to see them change. You can map their internal change using the Heart Plot. What if you're writing a long series? In those cases, give them a long runway. Walter White went from 'Mr Chips to Scarface' (Vince Gilligan, *Breaking Bad*). And make their flaw so entrenched it's unlikely to be fixed. Jimmy McGill might change almost everything about himself – name, appearance, office, but it's essentially all cosmetic.

A practical method for giving your protagonist enough time to change in a long-running series, is to have them start at the bottom of their chosen career. For example:

- **Mad Men (2007-15):** Peggy Olson goes from secretary to copywriter
- **Line of Duty (2012–):** Steve Arnott goes from Detective Sergeant to Detective Inspector
- **Succession (2018-2023):** Greg Hirsh goes from Logan's brother's grandson to Logan's great-nephew

Each of these characters has plenty of time to move their way up the greasy pole, whether it be in advertising, policing, or the family's media empire. Peggy joins the firm at the lowest tier – a secretary – and is a female in a male-dominated workplace. She's our window into the 1960s workplace. Through intelligent interventions, sacrifices, and suggestions, she climbs the ladder.

In *Line of Duty*, Steve Arnott is thrust into the world of AC-12 when his honesty about a failed operation puts him at odds with his colleagues. In *Succession*, Greg is barely a family member, but sneaks his way in after being fired from his job as an adventure park mascot. Each character is somewhat of an outsider, at odds with their new environment. But like plasticine, they mould themselves to fit in.

A simple way to check a protagonist has any of these traits is to use a simple checklist like the one in Table 10. Like many of the tables, you can use it to analyse an established protagonist, your own creation, or to help build a new one from scratch.

TRAIT	EXAMPLE/DETAIL
Interesting	
Selfless	
Relatable	
Want	
Need	
Superpower	
Flawed	
Active	
Fallible	
Resilient	
Malleable	

Table 10: Protagonist Trait Checklist.

Trait Tracking

If you want to track the traits of your protagonist through time, you can use a checklist, like the one I've created below (Table 11). Using it allows you to monitor the performance of your protagonist through the story. You can use it to check that your character does indeed display the characteristics you've so carefully crafted for them. A simple cross or tick in each box is often sufficient.

TRAIT	ACT 1 ACTION	ACT 2 ACTION	ACT 2B ACTION	ACT 2C ACTION	ACT 3C ACTION
Super-power					
Flaw					
Etc					

Table 11: Trait Tracking Table.

CHARACTER ARCS

A character arc describes the change (or not) a character undergoes from their first appearance to their last. While feature films usually focus on a single protagonist's arc, a TV series can follow more characters, e.g. *Game of Thrones*. That's not to say it's impossible in a feature film. For example, *Riders of Justice* ensures that each of the main character's arcs is fully realised. The musician Prince wanted each track of his songs to stand on its own. Every drumbeat, bass line, or vocal needed to be satisfying when soloed. Completing as many of your character arcs as you can is tough, but can be incredibly satisfying, especially if the arc is convincing.

The Queen's Gambit

This TV series is about an orphaned girl, Beth, who rises to the top of a competitive, male-dominated chess world. Each episode was structured as a Hero's Journey, with Beth as the protagonist. Following the template closely meant that she needed a mentor, new (or returning) friends and allies, and an antagonist for each episode. Many of the characters who appeared in early episodes returned in later ones, completing their arcs. Here's a summary:

- **Beth Harmon:** a drug-addicted, scruffy, no-hoper to a cleaned-up, glamorous chess champion
- **Jolene:** Beth's only friend at the orphanage who remains one at the end
- **Mr Shaibel:** gruff, rude, chess tutor is dead at the end, but through the press cuttings on his noticeboard, we discover he lovingly followed Beth's career

- **Biological parents:** Beth's biological father wants contact with her at the start but is denied by her mother, who later tries to kill Beth and herself
- **D.L. Townes:** early on, she shadows him. In the end, he's following her
- **Alma Wheatley:** Beth's adopted mother. She begins in good health but dies through alcoholism
- **Allston Wheatley:** her adopted father. Initially, he wants her but then ignores her. He hounds her when she's famous

Most of these character arcs show a significant change from start to finish. Many of the beginnings and endings are opposite of each other. It's not remarkably realistic that most would go through such an extraordinary shift but drama is heightened reality and stories are about change.

CHARACTER ARCHETYPES

A character archetype is an idealised person that completes a specific role in a story. They vary in form but perform the same function. I'll cover typical representations of the most commonly used but it's worth remembering that if the same persona is overused, they become stereotypes e.g. evil stepmother, gay best friend, and can become uninteresting or problematic. When the animation studio Pixar[6] started, they pledged never to use a

---

6. Pixar also created a story summary template:
   Once upon a time there was a _____
   Every day _____
   One day _____
   Because of that _____
   Because of that _____
   Until finally _____

wicked stepmother. But this doesn't mean it can't still be effective if done well, e.g. *Fleabag*. Much creativity can be applied when designing your character archetypes to subvert what we'd expect from them. You can also combine archetypes or switch characters from one to another. They provide helpful roles within stories and can help or hinder your protagonist.

The word archetype first appeared in the 1540s to refer to the source of a pattern, model, or type. Several hundred years later, Carl Jung, a Swiss psychiatrist, introduced the concept of psychological archetypes. He believed that history, culture, and personal context shaped them, and although limitless, a few kept recurring. Here's his list:

- The Hero
- The Child
- The Mother
- The Wise Old Man
- The Trickster
- The Eternal Boy
- The Cosmic Man
- The Artist-Scientist

Some of these will be familiar, others less so. Let's look at a couple of them. Like Peter Pan syndrome, the Eternal Boy is a child-God who is forever young. They're typically calm and wise, e.g. Godric in *True Blood*, but could also be an angry know-it-all, like Five, in *The Umbrella Academy*. The Cosmic Man is a benevolent male whose death seeds the world's creation. In some myths, the Cosmic Man is not just the beginning of life but its final state. This transformation echoes how the Jedi become one with the Force upon death (*Star Wars*) or how Grace Augustine merges with the Eywa in *Avatar*.

Many other scholars have created lists of character archetypes, and I encourage you to seek them out. Here's my list:

- The Hero
- The Mentor
- The Trickster
- The Everyman
- The Herald
- The Gatekeeper
- The Shadow
- The Outsider

It's shorter than many you'll find, but includes the most commonly used ones.

THE HERO

The Hero may or may not be the protagonist. They often are, as many stories follow the Hero's Journey, which moulds our protagonist into a hero. There's nothing wrong with this, and it doesn't mean our protagonist has to be heroic from the get-go like Perseus, Batwoman, or Flash Gordon. They can just as easily be Frank Gallagher (*Shameless*). The Hero archetype has specific traits: male, strong, heterosexual, risk-taking, and is a good fighter. This type of character is excellent in a scrape but there's a risk this archetype results in bland, outdated, misogynist characters. But, talented writers have succeeded in side-stepping the clichés. Let's look at some examples:

Superman

Perhaps the most obvious embodiment of the Hero archetype. He is one of the hardest to make more than just their brawn. However, by making him evil through tar-containing kryptonite (*Superman*) or Darkseid's intervention (*Batman v Superman*) or by focusing on his human persona and his life as a husband and father (*Superman and Lois*), his character has stayed fresh.

Peacemaker

The Peacemaker believes that killing is the best way to achieve peace. This series is a loud, action comedy that plays on the worst of the archetype's traits — stupidity, racism, and homophobia — to provide an opportunity for growth for the character. It does this by confronting Peacemaker with the type of people he'd typically despise and making him realise his backward views have come through ignorance, child abuse, and misinformation.

Dad's Army

In this show about the Home Guard in Britain during the Second World War, Lance Corporal Jack Jones is the Hero archetype (but not the protagonist). Jones is the local butcher who enlisted as a drummer boy at 14 and fought in both the Boer War and First World War. A true hero. But his age and shudders make him the least physically capable of the group. His heart's willing, but the body's failing.

Due to the Hero archetype's traits — brave and powerful, there's a risk they can overshadow the protagonist, so they need to be limited, as was done with Jones. In *The Boys*, Homelander is the all-American superhero but is, in fact, the villain. By keeping many of the archetype's traits — strength, flight, invulnerability, it makes him a terrifying antagonist.

THE MENTOR

The Mentor is a common archetype. Visible in most Hero's Journey type stories, the Mentor helps our protagonist reach their ultimate goal. The Mentor is the wisest of the wise, deducing what our protagonist needs to do to overcome their flaw. But the protagonist, naive and unwilling to change, ignores them. If they didn't, the Heart Plot would be over quickly, and the Mind Plot too. The protagonist needs to go through the process of failing due to their flaw before they are willing to address it. In the meantime, the Mentor will often train the protagonist to help them on their journey.

The role of Mentor as trainer lends itself to the movie montage. Whether it's karate, boxing, or playing chess, the inexperienced protagonist needs advice. In many stories, the Mentor is a wise older man or woman. They're often magical but all have expert knowledge and life experience to pass on.

Not all stories use this character archetype which makes the journey more challenging for our protagonist. Sometimes the Mentor dies, e.g. *The Queens' Gambit* or *Kingsman*, when their role has been fulfilled. In a long-running story, when the protagonist has become as skilled as the Mentor, their role changes, often becoming a friend. Or they may leave, only returning should the protagonist need assistance.

Gandalf

From *Lord of the Rings*, Gandalf is one of the most recognisable of all Mentors. He's a wise, magical, old gentleman who guides the four Hobbits on their journey. When Frodo wishes that the ring had never come to him, Gandalf tells him, 'So do all that live to see such times. But that is not for them to decide. All you have to do is to decide what you do with the time that is given to us.' In saying this, he's telling Frodo that heroes are made, not born.

Albert 'Al' Calavicci

In the original *Quantum Leap*, Sam Beckett endlessly leapfrogs through time, occupying other people's bodies at critical moments in their lives. After each jump, he receives guidance from Al, a colleague back in the laboratory, with access to a supercomputer called Ziggy. Al relayed Ziggy's predictions of what might happen if Sam made different choices. But they never knew how to get him home. Al shared the mentor role with Ziggy which gave his character the space to also be Sam's friend.

THE TRICKSTER

This character archetype is fun to write and can have dramatic effects on your story. The Trickster usually manifests itself as one of two types. The first is a fool who provides humour or pathos. They might become victims of their tall tales, such as Reginald 'Bubbles' Cousins in *The Wire*. He had the street smarts to help the police, but when he attempted to trick another addict, it had devastating consequences. The other type of Trickster is someone of high intellect, an overinflated ego or secret knowledge, which they use to tease or torment our protagonist. They might also be the antagonist, like The Riddler, taunting Batman with problems and puzzles. They're often able to shape-shift e.g. Mystique from the X-Men universe.

Loki

Loki originates from Norse mythology. He's a mischief-maker, shapeshifter and gender fluid. In the TV series *Loki*, he meets a female version of himself as well as several other forms. In Loki's initial appearances, he's the spoilt brother of the classic Hero archetype, Thor. Loki petulantly questions his father's decisions and undermines his beefcake brother. But when Thanos threatens to kill Thor, he sacrifices himself to try to save him. In the TV series, *Loki*, he is the protagonist. Being rebellious, he rails against authority – The Time Council – before being persuaded to work for them against a mysterious threat. However, when he meets it – Sylvie (female Loki) – he falls in love with her.

Magnifico Gigantic

In Isaac Asimov's *Foundation* books, Magnifico is a court jester. He's a deformed clown and appears to be of little importance. But Magnifico hides his ability to manipulate people with his mind. He uses his privileged position to take over the First Foundation – a library of all the universe's knowledge – a valuable resource when the Empire falls into chaos. Magnifico conquers planets and becomes supremely powerful. A team sets outs to find the Second Foundation to help end his reign. But Magnifico travels with them in disguise and nearly thwarts their plans.

THE EVERYMAN

The Everyman is the average human. They are like vanilla or printer paper, ordinary and commonplace. But this is what makes them so valuable to a story. They stand in for the audience, providing commentary on what's happening. This viewpoint is especially helpful when the story world is strange or inhuman. Although this character may face the same obstacles and adversities that a Hero archetype might, they will try to avoid conflict. Like all character archetypes, the Everyman can also be the protagonist. If they are, they take their traits with them, such as Arthur in *The Tick*, trying to stay out of heroing but being forced to lead the action.

Hugh 'Hughie' Campbell Jr.

The Boys is a comic book and TV series. Hughie joins The Boys – a team of primarily humans in a world where superhumans exist and appear heroic, but many are demonic. Hughie is regularly appalled by the behaviour of his teammates as well as The Seven – the most well-known but corrupt group of superheroes. Hughie's lack of superpowers makes him vulnerable. Hughie is a moderating influence on the leader of The Boys, William 'Billy' Butcher, who fulfils the Hero archetype. Hughie's character acts as a bridge between the absurdity of the behaviours of the super beings and their fawning public.

Penny

Penny is the neighbour of Leonard and Sheldon in *The Big Bang Theory*. She's a waitress and aspiring actress who becomes friends with the two physicists, along with their geeky friends. Her street smarts, lack of higher education, and belief in pseudoscience are a fun counterpoint to the nerds. Penny frequently asks them to dumb down complex science for her (and us). Penny helps them manage life outside the laboratory, from washing clothes to dating. In later series, Penny introduces their geeky girlfriends to girly behaviour. Penny does pick up some nerdy traits too but remains faithful to her Everyman (or Everywoman) archetype.

THE HERALD

The Herald archetype delivers an important message that often serves as the Inciting Incident. The Herald usually appears near the start and reveals important information. They can be a person, thing, or an object. The Herald is the letter inviting Cinderella to the ball, R2 D2 with Princess Leia's message for Obi-Wan Kenobi, or the words on a rock that states that only 'the true king' will be able to pull Excalibur from its clutches.

In most cases, the Herald is an object or person that deserves some reverence e.g. a high-ranking individual. In *300*, Xeres sends three Heralds to the Spartans to demand their surrender. They're thrown into a pit. The Herald's request might not always be genuine. To try to catch Robin Hood, the Sheriff of Nottingham organises an archery contest with valuable prizes, knowing that Robin won't be able to resist entering.

Witches

In most versions of *Macbeth*, a trio of female witches' prophesies to the victorious General that he will ascend to the throne of Scotland. Subsequent events appear to support this prediction, and Macbeth, with the support of his wife, plots his way to power but, ultimately, to their deaths.

THE GATEKEEPER

The Gatekeeper acts as an obstacle to the protagonist entering somewhere. They test the protagonist's commitment to their cause. This interaction often occurs at the transitions between Acts, as our protagonist moves from one world to another. The Gatekeeper's role is to keep the unworthy from entering or prevent the protagonist from reaching their goal. Like the Herald, they take many forms, often animalistic e.g. the spider-like Boiler Geezer in *Spirited Away*. Cerebus was a multi-headed dog that guarded the gates of the Underworld and was captured by Heracles. In the *Wizard of Oz*, Dorothy must get past a fastidious doorkeeper to enter the Emerald City. In *The Batman*, twin bouncers guard Club Penguin which both Bruce and Batman must get past.

Heimdall

In North mythology, Heimdall is a god who watches for intruders at the junction of Bifröst (the rainbow bridge) and the sky – the route into Asgard. He is all-seeing and all-hearing and has a fractious relationship with Loki and Thor. Sometimes he battles Thor to prevent him from entering or leaving Asgard. Other times, he assists Thor in saving the people of Asgard.

THE SHADOW

The Shadow is usually the antagonist and the primary opposing force, preventing our protagonist from reaching their goal. The Shadow is called such as it's so closely twinned to our protagonist. **Me and my shadow**. And like a shadow, they're a darker, more amorphous version, and usually responsible for the threat to the protagonist's Home World.

Like all archetypes, the Shadow needn't be human (e.g. a shark) or even alive (e.g. an asteroid). It could even be internal (e.g. addiction). However, it's usually a single entity that the protagonist must confront by the end. There might be defeated minions on the way, but ultimately, the story usually finishes with a showdown between them. The Shadow doesn't typically consider themselves the villain and believes their actions to be justified. Thanos truly believes that killing half the universe is better than the risk of losing everyone. This belief makes him a tragic, empathetic figure.

The Shadow is often a mirror opposite of the protagonist. This is most clearly seen in superhero movies, where flaws and weaknesses are boldly apparent. While Superman has superhuman powers, Lex Luther has none. While Superman has average smarts, Lex is highly intelligent. Batman is calm, considered and dressed in black; the Joker is a laughing, colourful ball of chaos.

In more **realistic** stories, the Shadow's more nuanced. For example, in *Sound of Metal*, the Shadow is Lou's father. Although opposed to her leaving with Ruben after her mother's death, he accepts it was the right thing for her to do but now believes she should stay with him.

In some stories, the Shadow is an evil copy of the protagonist. So rather than opposite traits, they're similar. In *Hulk*, Bruce's father becomes a larger, seemingly more powerful version of his son's alter ego. Bruce doesn't want his powers as they've brought him only trouble. When his father offers to take them, he's tempted. But he realises he must keep them, to prevent creatures like his father from doing harm.

In *Logan*, Wolverine faces X-24, a younger version of himself. Logan, the original Weapon X, was designed to be a killer and has fought against that programming all his life. Weapon X wants to kill, while Logan doesn't unless protecting the innocent.

To help design your antagonist (or your protagonist), it can be helpful to list their traits side by side (Table 12). It's a quick way to help generate some character traits to fill out either or both of your characters. And it's good to remember they can be opposite, the same or just different. But if they're the same, there needs to be something else driving the conflict e.g. misunderstanding, philosophical differences, or manipulation.

In many stories, the protagonist and the Shadow want opposing outcomes. Batman wants order, the Joker chaos. Thanos wants to wipe out half the universe; the Avengers don't. Jake Gettes wants to prevent a repeat of what happened in Chinatown, but he's doomed to repeat himself. In other stories, the protagonist and Shadow want the same thing. Sometimes it's a physical object, like the Lektor decoder in *For Your Eyes Only* or the Ark of the Covenant in *Raiders of The Lost Ark*. In the *The Godfather*, it's to be the most powerful mafia family. To summarise:

1. The protagonist and the antagonist want **different** things, but they can't both have them
2. The protagonist and the antagonist want the **same** thing, but both can't have it

The two scenarios create conflict. In the play *John*, Jenny and Elias, a couple, spend a weekend in a quaint Bed and Breakfast and agonise over their relationship. They never reach a solution that suits both of them. Jenny wants her partner and her lover. Elias wants her to himself. In *West Side Story*, the Sharks and the Jets both want to control the neighbourhood they share and won't accept the other having superiority.

PROTAGONIST (SPIDERMAN)	ANTAGONIST (RHINO)
Slim with fabric suit	Bulky, with metal suit
American	Russian
Small, agile	Big, slower
Student	Mobster

Table 12: Protagonist-Antagonist Table.

THE OUTSIDER

Unlike the character archetypes above, which appear in many stories, the Outsider is less common. But it's such a powerful one that it's worthy of inclusion. The Outsider has traits in common with the Everyman. They can also comment on what is happening – pointing out what's unique or unusual. But unlike the Everyman, rather than being ordinary, they're extraordinary e.g. Spock, Data, or Seven of Nine (Star Trek universe). Each of them is part human and will often comment on the strangeness of human behaviour.

In other stories, the Outsider is less benign e.g. *The Man Who Fell to Earth*, *The Day the Earth Stood Still*, *Under the Skin*. This allows them more freedom and they can utilise their otherworldliness to manipulate or disrupt human behaviour.

When the Outsider is the protagonist, they manifest as a wanderer. Examples include Blondie in *The Good, the Bad and the Ugly* or the lead characters in the TV series *The Incredible Hulk*, *Kung Fu*, and *Reacher*.

The Outsider is a powerful trope, perhaps because it reflects our experiences of being one, e.g. moving home or attending a new school.

USING CHARACTER ARCHETYPES

Consider carefully if, how, and when you will use character archetypes. You could use the archetypes to help create characters or you could use a table (Table 13) to assign existing characters to better define them. It might inspire you to subvert expectations, e.g. make the mentor a child (John Connor in *Terminator 2: Judgment Day*) or switch gender (*Russian Doll*). You might choose to leave one or more out, have characters with multiple traits, or have them switch from one to another. In *To Kill a Mockingbird*, Atticus Finch has elements of three: Father, Hero, and the Idealist.

Symbolic Archetypes

Symbolic archetypes are colours, elements, or shapes. They act as a visual association to something deep-rooted in our psyche. For example, we associate yellow with daytime or warmth, presumably due to its strong association with sunshine and fire. Likewise, we'd probably make a mental link between green and nature. Often, the colour's in the form of a light source. A glowing white or yellow light might suggest a god-like presence or an awakening. An absence of light might indicate danger or death. The natural elements provide good symbolic archetypes. Rain often indicates depression or sadness. A gust of wind, approaching jeopardy.

Shapes can be symbolic archetypes. The 'S' on Superman's costume is reassuring. Batman's night signal is, 'not just a call; it's a warning' (*The Batman*). Square rooms or straight lines suggest conformity or entrapment, like the corridors in *Severance*. A circle feels more harmonious; arches make grand entrances. You can also play against symbolic archetypes, such as Charlie and Carrie kissing in the rain (*Four Weddings and a Funeral*) or Don Lockwood dancing in it (*Singing in the Rain*).

ARCHETYPE	DESCRIPTION	CHARACTER
Hero	Transformative, self-sacrificing, flawed	
Mentor	Teacher, gift giver, conscience, motivator	
Threshold guardian	Guards, lieutenants, foe or ally, gatekeepers	
Herald	Issue challenges, announces need for change	
Shapeshifter	Change appearance/mood, changeable	
Shadow	Dark side, antagonist	
Ally	Friend, buddy, pet, sidekick, servant	
Trickster	Comic relief, catalysts	

Table 13: Character Archetype.

Setting Archetypes

The story's location can cue the audience into a desired mood or feeling. Would The *Blair Witch Project* have worked as well if the movie hadn't been set in a forest at night time? We associate certain places with being more dangerous. In *The Wizard of Oz*, Dorothy, Toto, the Tin Man, Scarecrow, and the Lion go through The Haunted Forest and are attacked by flying monkeys. In *The Vorrh*, the forest of the same name is vast, and perhaps neverending, full of good and evil monsters.

The dark grandeur of Gotham feels like a fitting place for a Dark Knight, just as Camelot is a worthy place for more traditional knights. Islands are popular setting archetypes, suggesting secrecy or isolation. They're often the lair of a James Bond nemesis. Often explorers will land on them, either planned (*Sinbad and the Eye of the Tiger*, *Pirates of the Caribbean*) or unplanned (*Lost*, *Castaway*).

Object Archetypes

Objects have meaning. This association may be through their function, e.g. a key is used to open a door, but can be less specific, e.g. representing discovery. In *The Matrix*, the Key Master has physical keys that unlock doors but they're really passcodes to access the Source (the central computing core for the machine mainframe in *The Matrix*). A ring suggests devotion or commitment. In the *Lord of the Rings*, wearing the One Ring is all consuming, and while Gollum (previously Sméagol) outlives any other Hobbit, it deforms his body and twists his mind. Swords, whether made of metal or light, signify valour or elevated status. *The Sandman* has three object archetypes: a pouch of dream sand, a ruby, and a helmet.

Ordinary objects become archetypes if given a personal or spiritual connection. Indiana Jones seeks the Ark of the Covenant in *Raiders of the Lost Ark*. In *Russian Doll*, Nadia wears a gold Russian coin necklace, once worn by her dead mother. In *No Time to Die*, Bond gives his blue jumper to his daughter. The objects become sacred through their provenance. We can see this power in non-fiction too e.g. *The Repair Shop*, where broken things have emotional resonance due to their connection to a lost friend or relative.

BIG CHARACTERS

Some characters are significant by design; others seem to outgrow their status. In *Pulp Fiction*, Maurice is not shown face-on until the scene where Butch runs him over. This deliberate obfuscation of the antagonist builds him up into a more frightening figure.

Other characters become so iconic, they seem to transcend the stories they are in e.g. Blanche Dubois from *A Streetcar Named Desire*, Darth Vader, Kramer, or Johnny 'Rooster' Byron from *Jerusalem*.

Some that break out are neither the protagonist nor the antagonist. Instead, they're often friends of the main character, such as Gene Hunt from *Life on Mars*, Poe from *Altered Carbon*, or Saul Goodman from *Breaking Bad*. They sometimes outlive the protagonist.

What makes these big characters so unique? Here are some reasons:

- They often enter the story late
- Have mythological qualities
- Have a catchphrase
- Span several character archetypes
- Represent the theme, time, or world of the story

Wolverine

Wolverine is a character that began in comics and TV but is best known for being a member of the X-Men. He has mythological qualities by being nearly immortal. Like all superheroes, he has unique skills and has a sharp turn of phrase. He spans several archetypes: Hero, Outsider, Mentor, Carer, and Father. He also represents the fight of minorities seeking acceptance.

Gene Hunt

Gene Hunt was the incumbent detective in the series *Life on Mars*. When Sam Tyler is thrown back 33 years in time, he finds himself partnered with Gene. Gene has a mythological status due to the reverence afforded to him by his strait-laced colleagues. He has a unique sartorial dress and a cool car. He also has an impressive turn of phrase: 'Gene Hunt. Your DCI. And it's 1973. Almost dinner time. I'm having hoops'; 'You know, if you were Pinocchio, you'd have just poked my eye out'; or 'He's got fingers in more pies than a leper on a cookery course.'

WHO'S THE HERO?

Although it's almost always obvious who the protagonist is of your story, it may be worth checking. Repositioning less typical characters as the protagonist can reap dividends, e.g. *The Joker*. I'll now demonstrate this by example, using *Dracula*.

In the book, Jonathan travels to Transylvania to meet Dracula. After their encounter, he's not seen for half the book as the story switches back to England. On Jonathan's return, he meets a vampire-hunting team, including a mentor figure, Van Helsing. Dracula then arrives in London, depositing coffins across the city. Bats and wolves are seen at night, and children are attacked. Dracula turns Jonathan's Home World into somewhere dangerous (Alien World). If I summarise *Dracula*, with Jonathan as the traditional protagonist, we get something like this.

- Jonathan leaves his ordinary world
- He meets Dracula and wants to defeat him
- He fails and returns home
- Back in London, Jonathan meets Van Helsing
- Jonathan joins the team of vampire hunters
- Mina has been compromised; they spoil Dracula's coffins

- They kill the Brides of Dracula
- They find Dracula's resting place but he's escaped
- They travel to Transylvania
- They find and kill Dracula
- The curse on Mina ends

In prose form:

Jonathan leaves his home world of London and meets Dracula. Realising his malice, he plans to kill him, but fails. Jonathan escapes Transylvania and returns to London, where he joins a vampire hunting team led by Van Helsing. Dracula arrives in London and puts Jonathan's wife, Mina, under his spell. The team kill Dracula's Brides and destroy his coffins. Dracula escapes. They travel to Transylvania and kill him, ending the curse on Mina.

As written, it has many elements of the Hero's Journey. But Jonathan's long absence in the middle makes it an oddly constructed novel. What if Dracula was the protagonist?

Dracula lives in his isolated castle, a recluse due to his disabling biology. He's childlike and keen to learn about the world. Inspired by his invited teacher, Jonathan, he travels to London. He learns the ways of this new world. Van Helsing, his antagonist, discovers his arrival and seeks to destroy him with help from Jonathan. Dracula dodges his pursuers and recruits one of their own to his side. The team kill his wives and destroy his sleeping places. He flees to Transylvania where they track him down and kill him.

I think this demonstrates the flexibility of the Hero's Journey, or stories in general, and how, with enough skill, even the evillest of characters can feel empathetic.

WEBS

Using characters to reflect different point of views (POVs) of the theme is a great way to examine it and make your characters more distinct. A parallel technique is to create a web of association based on your protagonist (or antagonist). This clarifies what each character means to them. In addition, you can use it to find connections between secondary characters. Here's an example:

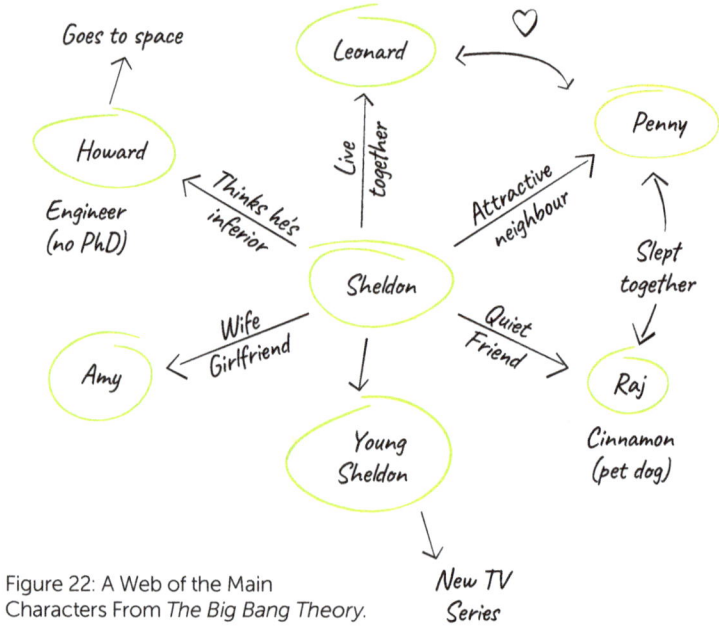

Figure 22: A Web of the Main Characters From *The Big Bang Theory*.

This tool is particularly handy when trying to squeeze as much story from a few characters e.g. soaps or sitcoms. Other forms can benefit to, particularly those that are centred on families e.g. *Succession*.

POINT OF VIEW

This section is about point of view (POV). Once the protagonist is set, the story is normally told from their POV. This doesn't mean you can't jump into different people's heads or have scenes without the protagonist, but it's rare, especially in a feature film. This makes the protagonist by default the hero in the Hero's Journey. But this doesn't mean everyone else in the story considers them heroic.

The antagonist, their shadow, will likely consider them an obstacle or a nuisance. They may considers **themselves** a hero. In comedy, the protagonist is usually a larger-than-life figure with peculiar characteristics. Whether it be Mr Bean's lack of speech or Inspector Clouseau's clumsiness, they make a lasting impression in any situation. And this is where much of the humour comes from – their behaviour and the reaction of others to it. If any of these characters existed in the real world, they'd be intolerable. Their colleagues would have left the organisation and neighbours would've moved away. But one of the benefits of sitcoms, where most of these **monsters** reside, is that there's no escape.

Let's use David Brent from *The Office* to examine both POV and **also** perception.

David Brent's Self-View

- Makes dreams come true
- Funny
- A friend, boss, entertainer
- Rock and Roll
- A disciple spreading his message

Colleagues' View of David Brent

- Gareth idolises David
- Tim, David's shadow, both likes and despises David
- Dawn calls him a 'sad little man' after a practical joke
- Neil thinks he's underperforming

How David Brent Thinks Others See Him

- Friend
- Mentor
- Humorous
- Entertaining

David thinks others see him the same way as he sees himself. This lack of self-awareness is what helps the character stay the same.

REVELATIONS

In *The Office*, the other characters complement David Brent. They reveal the different sides of our protagonist when they push, poke, tease, complement, and irritate our protagonist. By doing so, they help to create a more rounded protagonist.

Murderbot is the main character in a series of sci-fi books by Martha Wells. It puts you in the head of a sitcom-loving security robot, with a dark past, that wants to be more autonomous. It's part biological so has some limited emotions. Its personality appears unique, which may be related to the trauma of its past indiscretion and memory reset. It's shy and introverted. Its interactions with others reveal its personality and views on life:

- Mensah is one of Murderbot's employers. She is human, caring, and thoughtful, and persuades Murderbot that showing emotions (facial expressions) can be helpful
- ART is an intelligent, aggressive, fast spaceship that doesn't understand human emotions. It values Murderbot's ability to do so and considers them friends
- Miki is a pet-like robot. Murderbot's wish to be autonomous is emphasised by Murderbot's disparaging views of Miki's obsequence to humans

When writing secondary characters, consider how their relationship to the protagonist can reveal more about our hero.

FLAW

Every person and every character has flaws. However, what others perceive as your flaws, you may see as strengths. Most of David Brent's co-workers find his attempts at humour irritating, but he sees them as an asset.

All protagonists need a central flaw. This flaw will hamper their attempts at reaching their goal. With each shot at getting closer, their fault will disrupt their progress. Each failed attempt will wear down their resistance to addressing it.

Eventually, our protagonist should realise they must overcome their flaw to help them get what they need, which may also help them get what they want.

Why is the flaw so challenging to overcome? The reason is that it's deeply ingrained in our protagonist's psyche, often since childhood. For many writers, defining it and incorporating it is challenging. It's certainly the part I find the most challenging. For that reason, I created this diagram:

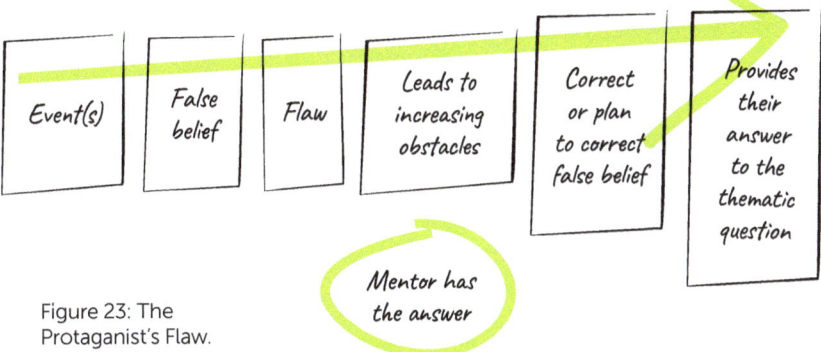

Figure 23: The Protaganist's Flaw.

If this process-driven approach to creating a flaw is too difficult, just create a flaw and forget the rest. Unless you plan to write a story with a protagonist from childbirth to adulthood, or use flashbacks, we don't need to see the flaw's origin. But it's reveal can be extremely powerful e.g. when we discover why Elinor Oliphant behaves (and looks) the way she does (*Elinor Oliphant is Completely Fine*).

The trauma that the protagonist has experienced creates a **false belief system**. It doesn't have to be painful, just impactful. Perhaps their mother tells them men can't be trusted when their father leaves for another woman. They believe it and carry this with them into adulthood. Create a false belief system that affects their behaviour in multiple situations and is hard to break down.

A list of flaws is included in Appendix 1. Some appear to be minor, e.g. timid and others, major, e.g. megalomaniac. Seemingly minor flaws in the right genre, e.g. comedy, can be extremely effective.

Once you have a flaw in mind, you can envisage how it will make your protagonist's journey difficult. Not every obstacle needs to challenge the flaw, but many should. There needs to be enough instances where they can no longer bear the failure and must address their flaw's origin. Only in this painful self-examination will they be able to examine the core belief and realise it's false. Once this realisation dawns on them, they can dismiss it, changing them forever and freeing them from its pernicious influence. Two examples:

Beth Harmon — The Queen's Gambit

Beth feels unloved due to being abandoned by her parents and growing up in an harsh orphanage. She turns this rejection into a belief that she's unlovable, so there's no point in loving anyone else. Throughout Beth's life, she is aloof and doesn't form any lasting relationships, except with drugs and alcohol. Her adopted mother is more of a surrogate older sister, using Beth to have fun with, while her husband is away.

When successful, Beth returns to the orphanage and visits the basement. She realises that there **was** someone who loved her: Mr Shaibel, who had followed every step of her career. He loved her unconditionally (even when she had been to rude him) and showed her discipline (like a parent). Beth quits drinking and allows her rivals to support her in her biggest match. She realises that she can still visualise the game, even without tranquillisers.

Ruben Stone – The Sound of Metal

Ruben is a ball of energy, moving from gig to gig with his troubled girlfriend in a silver motorhome. He never knew who his father was and his mother, an army medic, drove them from country to country. Ruben's a recovering drug addict. He believes forward motion is the best way to stay ahead of his demons. When Ruben is forced to stay in one place, it's a monumental struggle. He does everything he can to return things (hearing, relationship) to normal and get back on the road. However, his inability to stay still makes his recovery nigh impossible.

When Ruben realises that going on the road again will harm his girlfriend, Lou, he addresses his flaw. While he might be willing to sacrifice his own well-being, he's not going to hurt her. Ruben ends their relationship. With the false belief that moving forward is the secret to being safe and loved dismantled, he can now stop. He finds inner peace.

When our protagonist corrects their flaw they answer the thematic question. If you remember back to Aristotle's formula: hypothesis > antithesis > synthesis, we've reached synthesis. Our protagonist spent the first two Acts demonstrating his hypothesis through words and deeds, while the antagonist opposed them. At the end, we have the answer to the thematic question – a mixture of both their points of view.

The Queen's Gambit

- **Thematic question:** 'Can someone unloved as a child be loved as an adult?'
- **Hypothesis (Beth):** 'No.'
- **Antithesis (friends/lovers/mentor):** 'Yes.'
- **Synthesis:** 'Yes, if I let them in.'

The solution's embodied in Beth's decision not to leave Moscow straight away, but spend time with her fans.

The Sound of Metal

- **Thematic question:** 'Can you be at peace if not moving forward?'
- **Hypothesis (Ruben):** 'No.'
- **Antithesis (Joe):** 'Yes.'
- **Synthesis:** 'Yes, but it takes work.'

Ruben removes his hearing implants, controls his breathing, and takes in the scenery.

POSITIVE FLAW

There are certain stories where the protagonist's flaw is positive. It's positive in a sense that the behaviour they exhibit that holds them back would objectively be seen by most as admirable.

In *Whiplash*, Johnny is a loving son, who always has time for his family. But his tutor tells him that to be the ultimate drummer, supreme sacrifices need to be made. Johnny resists and resists until he realises that to fulfil that dream, he must reject his family. This is embodied when he dismisses his father before the final performance.

In the horror *Midsommar*, Dani is the dutiful friend and girlfriend, sublimating herself to others' wishes. They travel to rural Sweden for a festival and find themselves in the clutches of a cult. She's dragged from one nightmare to another, before deciding to take control and be in charge. If she must live in hell, she might as well be the devil.

In the play, *The Girl Who Was Very Good at Lying*, the protagonist is gleeful about her skill for lying, and uses it to get what she wants. But then she comes up against someone even better than she is, and loses, it's devastating. So she tells the truth, and begins a new dawn, naked and reborn.

NOTES

EXTRAS

In this final section, I pull together a few tips and tricks that don't quite fit anywhere else.

EDITING

Plot Versus Character

The eternal battle. While you might debate which comes first, like the chicken or the egg, we can agree that both are important in telling a good story. In contrast, great characters remain long in the memory and can form widely circulated memes. But the plot gives them something to do and a route for change. Aristotle felt that plot was more important. Even though he didn't like *deus ex machina*,[7] his stories were full of well-known characters. Much like many cinema releases, his characters arrived fully formed and were often inhuman. A method of checking the balance between plot and character in your stories is to use God Mode and Player Mode.

God Mode

In this technique, you put on a metaphysical cap and become a god. You are now external to the story. You can direct your characters like chess pieces. You control the weather. And time. Everything. You can imagine what would happen if someone did something to someone else and then made it happen.

One way to practise this is to consider one of your favourite TV characters. Someone you feel you know inside and out. If they're from a soap or long-running TV show, even better. As for most of these, their world is a single or similar locations. What if you put them somewhere else? Or they made a different decision from one we know? E.g. what would the Square look like if Dirty

---

7. Deus ex machina is a plot device used to solve an impossible plot situation through an unlikely or unbelievable occurrence.

Den hadn't divorced Angie (*EastEnders*)? In this mindset, you focus on what is happening. Does other stuff need to happen around the protagonist? Does a scene move the plot forward? Do the characters learn something?

Player Mode

In this scenario, you embody your characters. You feel what they feel and do what they do. You could literally mimic their situation and improvise what they might do next. For example, turn off the lights if they're in the dark. How do you feel? What do you instinctively want to do next? Shout out? Find the light switch? If your character's hungry, skip a meal.

Write the scene from their POV. You could write a synopsis of the whole story from their perspective. It can reveal things you hadn't realised they might be thinking or feeling. Player mode allows you to consider if the character would do something as written. Sometimes when I'm in the zone, my protagonist appears to *choose* what to do next with no conscious instruction on my part.

Other Techniques to Consider

Read your work backwards, line by line. Hard to do, but an excellent way to pick up spelling errors. Another is to read a single character's dialogue from start to finish. By doing this, you can check for consistency. Perhaps he has a favourite phrase, e.g. 'Fuck off!' (Logan from *Succession*) that you might want to check is not over or under-used. Maybe they use short or long sentences? Do they use rhetorical questions? Or slang?

Whatever editing techniques you choose to use, they should help to ensure you stay true to your story and your characters.

DETECTIVES

All stories are detective stories. They're about our protagonist finding out what's damaging their world and what's eating them up inside. But that's not really what this section is about. It's about detectives: coppers, sleuths, and investigators.

Detectives are a popular TV subject, often in the form of a case of the week, whether it be a seemingly unsolvable crime, e.g. *Ironside* or a strange occurrence, e.g. *Mulder and Scully*. They're often based in a precinct, so have colleagues e.g. *Brooklyn Nine-Nine*. This gives them longevity. This doesn't mean they have to be ageless. Indeed, many a b-story in the Rebus books revolves around his changing personal life.

Detectives have flaws, e.g. alcoholic, scruffy, or aloof which makes things more challenging. But their flaws are not explicitly related to an inner need, and are rarely fixed. If the investigator fixed their flaws, that would be the end of the crime-fighting career, e.g. *The Dark Knight Rises*.

TV VS FILM

For most of those reading this section, you've probably started or completed a first feature or TV pilot so understand the differences. But let's pause to reflect on them.

Firstly, TV relies more on characters than plot. This bias is due to the longer time we spend with a series and the fact that we remember characters more than the plot (hence the recaps). So go big with your characters in your TV pilot. Make them as bold as you can – especially if it's a sitcom – then pull them back only when they become unbelievable.

With film, even with increasing running times, the plot is usually as, or more, important as the characters. You need a character that's quick to get. That's why action movies with established IP work so well. We all know who Batman is (or should do!).

That doesn't mean exceptions can't work e.g. *Nomadland*, *Coda*, but it takes a highly skilled team to pull it off. Films also tend to hold more strictly to the Hero's Journey. Despite the diminishing differences, they still exist.

LOSS

Loss is a recurrent element in stories and is usually tied to the protagonist (or antagonist) like a millstone around their necks. Sometimes loss is the story's theme. Other times, it's associated with the Significant Death point. Frequently, the loss of someone or something is a wound that hasn't healed and drives our character's behaviour, e.g. Thanos.

In the film *Shadow*, Captain Tian deliberately keeps a wound in his chest fresh to remind him of his lost home city. Misaki deliberately chooses to leave the scar on her cheek unfixed (*Drive My Car*). In *Nomadland*, Fern has lost almost everything: her work, home, and community. She's a wandering soul who finds community with others, equally adrift from society. In *The Peanut Butter Falcon*, it's Tyler's older brother. In *Elinor Oliphant is Completely Fine*, it's her sister. Some others:

- **The Father:** loss of a daughter (past) and loss of one's mind (present and future)
- **Promising Young Woman:** loss of a best friend (past) and loss of the will to live (present)
- **Sound of Metal:** loss of hearing (present) and purpose (present and future)
- **Aftersun**: the memory of a lost parent

Why is loss such a powerful tool? Peter Marris, the sociologist, believes that understanding loss and its consequences (grief) helps us understand change. And change is the engine that drives our protagonist's journey. Some writers use the Grief Cycle –

a series of states most humans experience after a loss – as a structure for stories.

Peter said that the loss of something is a loss of meaning which disrupts our ability to make sense of life. This breakdown is similar to what happens in the Heart Plot. Our protagonist reaches a point where they can't cope anymore. They must face their flaw. Only through its acceptance can they recover and move on. And similarly, only through acceptance that loss is a part of life, such as that often occurs at the Significant Death point of the Hero's Journey, can the protagonist enter their final Act.

EXPOSITION

Exposition is a necessary evil. Since the *Star Wars* films have monopolised the scrolling text method, you'll need to find another way. Sci-fi gets a pass more generally – due to its complexity. A voice over is often used, to describe the world as it is.

Other methods are needed for other genres. The Everyman is one way, asking questions for someone else to answer. Or you could use TV broadcasts, newspaper headlines, or billboards. Another is to hide it within an argument. By weaponising exposition, it becomes more digestible. Another technique, often used by Marvel, is to deliver exposition after an action scene when the characters (and us) pause for breath.

SCREENWRITING FORMAT

The best way to learn about screenwriting format is to look at the scripts of produced screenplays. By reading them, you'll also learn a lot about writing them. But here are some general tips:

A new scene involves a change of time or location. A typical screenplay has double the number of scenes to pages. Some scenes may be no more than a single shot. The golden rule of scenes is to

get in late and get out early. You don't need to see someone walk up to a lift, push a button, wait, and then get in, if the critical action happens halfway up, when the lift gets stuck. Here's a handy check list:

- Bold the scene description
- Keep action/slug lines to three or fewer. If you need more, start another block
- Begin with a physical object – a cue to what may come next or a misdirection
- Character descriptions: age, gender plus a few adjectives to describe them, e.g. tall with glasses, big but gentle. The best descriptors often are non-physical e.g. never sits still or anger burns through their eyes
- Present tense
- Put the reader into the scene
- Scenes should flow from one to another
- Finish with something that naturally moves us onto the next scene

LOGLINES

Loglines are a crucial tool to help concisely pitch your story. There are several formats you can use. Here are the ones I use:

Protagonist + struggle with Antagonist + what's at stake

Here we have the protagonist, their antagonist and what's at stake. This template is good for describing simplistic, high-stakes stories. E.g. *Duel*, 'A business commuter is pursued and terrorised by the malevolent driver of a massive truck'.

We can include the Inciting Incident:

Protagonist + Inciting Incident + Protagonist's goal + central conflict

In this one, we also know what the protagonist wants and why it's going to be hard to get it. These loglines often start with 'When...' e.g. 'When a town sheriff investigates the mutilated body of a swimmer, he realises that to protect the townsfolk he'll have to go to sea and hunt a killer shark.'

A more expansive alternative is:

In a (Setting), a (Flawed) (Protagonist) has a (Problem) (caused by an Antagonist) and (faces Conflict) as they try (to achieve a Goal).

More formulaic than the other two, this incorporates the starting location and the protagonist's flaw. The inclusion of the location is helpful if it's not present-day or is particularly important, e.g. outer space. This version also includes the flaw – particularly useful if their weakness can be summed up in one word (and links to the challenges they'll face). For example, Brody faces extra difficulties because he's scared of water. This format also includes the antagonist more precisely than the others.

And finally:

In a (Setting), one or more (Flawed) (Protagonists) want something but face conflict from one or more (Antagonists) as they try to achieve it and find out they need something else.

This one allows for more than one protagonist, e.g. *Thelma and Louise*, as well as one or more antagonists. It also includes the Mind and Heart plots. Although it may not reveal whether they get what they want, it does tell us what they need. This inclusion also gives us a clue to the theme of the story.

NOTES

APPENDIX

247

BIBLIOGRAPHY

FILMS

127 Hours, 2010, Danny Boyle, Simon Beaufoy, Aron Ralston
1917, 2019, Sam Mendes, Krysty Wilson-Cairns
3:10 to Yuma, 2007, Halsted Welles, Michael Brandt, Derek Haas
300, 2006, Zack Snyder, Kurt Johnstad, Michael B. Gordon
A Few Good Men, 1992, Aaron Sorkin
A Grand Day Out, 1989, Nick Park, Steve Rushton
Aftersun, 2022, Charlotte Wells
Alien, 1979, Dan O'Bannon, Ronald Shusett
Another Round, 2020, Thomas Vinterberg, Tobias Lindholm
Assault on Precinct 13, 2005, John Carpenter, James DeMonaco
Atomic Blonde, 2017, Kurt Johnstad, Antony Johnston, Sam Hart
Avatar, 2009, James Cameron
Avengers: Infinity War, 2018, Christopher Markus, Stephen McFeely
Batman v Superman: Dawn of Justice, 2016, Bob Kane, Bill Finger, Jerry Siegel
Belfast, 2021, Kenneth Branagh
Beyond the Infinite Two Minutes, 2020, Makoto Ueda
Blade Runner, 1982, Hampton Fancher, David Webb Peoples, Philip K. Dick
Blazing Saddles, 1974, Mel Brooks, Norman Steinberg, Andrew Bergman, Richard Pryor, Alan Uger
Boiling Point, 2021, Philip Barantini, James Cummings
Born on the Fourth of July, 1989, Oliver Stone, Ron Kovic
Brian and Charles, 2022, David Earl, Chris Hayward
Brief Encounter, 1945, Noel Coward, Anthony Havelock-Allan, David Lean, Ronald Neame
Bullet Train, 2020, Zak Olkewicz, Kotaro Isaka
Butch Cassidy and the Sundance Kid, 1969, William Goldman
Cars, 2006, John Lasseter, Joe Ranft, Jorgen Klubien, Dan Fogelman, Kiel Murray, Phil Lorin
Castaway, 2000, William Broyles Jr.
Chinatown, 1974, Robert Towne, Roman Polanski
City Slickers, 1991, Lowell Ganz, Babaloo Mandel
Close Encounters of the Third Kind, 1977, Steven Spielberg, Hal Barwood, Jerry Belson, John Hill, Matthew Robbins
Cloverfield, 2008, Drew Goddard
Coda, 2021, Sian Heder
Collateral, 2004, Stuart Beattie
Compartment No. 6, 2021, Andris Feldmanis, Juho Kuosmanen, Rosa Liksom
Dances with Wolves, 1990, Michael Blake
Deathloop, 2021, Joe Feilder
Death on the Nile, 2022, Michael Green, Agatha Christie

Die Hard, 1988, Roderick Thorp, Jeb Stuart, Steven E. de Souza
Dirty Harry, 1971, Harry Julian Fink, Rita M. Fink, Dean Reisner, Terence Malick, Jo Heims, John Milius
Don't Look Up, 2021, Adam McKay, David Sirota
Drive My Car, 2021, Haruki Murakami, Ryusuke Hamaguchi, Takamusa Oe
Duel, 1971, Richard Matheson
Dune, 2021, Jon Spaihts, Denis Villeneuve, Eric Roth, Frank Herbert
Edge of Tomorrow, 2014, Christopher McQuarrie, Jez Butterworth, John-Henry Butterworth
Everything Everywhere All at Once, 2022, Daniel Kwan, David Scheinert
Finding Nemo, 2003, Andrew Stanton, Bob Peterson, David Reynolds
First Man, 2018, Josh Singer, James R. Hansen
For Your Eyes Only, 1981, Richard Maibaum, Michael G. Wilson, Ian Fleming
Forrest Gump, 1994, Winston Groom, Eric Roth
Four Weddings and a Funeral, 1994, Richard Curtis
Get Out, 2017, Jordan Peele
Goldfinger, 1964, Richard Maibaum, Paul Dehn, Ian Fleming
Good, 2008, C. P. Taylor, John Wrathall
GoodFellas, 1990, Nicolas Pileggi, Martin Scorcese
Guardians of the Galaxy, 2014, James Gunn, Nicole Perlman, Dan Abnett, Andy Lanning
Hidden Figures, 2016, Allison Schroeder, Theodore Melfi, Margot Lee Shetterly
Hulk, 2003, Stan Lee, Jack Kirby, James Schumas, John Turman, Michael France
I am Mother, 2019, Michael Lloyd Green, Grant Sputore
Independence Day, 1996, Dean Devlin, Roland Emmerich
Jaws, 1975, Peter Benchley, Carl Gottlieb
John Wick, 2014, Derek Kolstad
Jojo Rabbit, 2019, Christine Leunens, Taika Waititi
Joker, 2019, Todd Phillips, Scott Silver, Bob Kane, Bill Finger, Jerry Robinson
Judge Dredd, 1995, John Wagner, Carlos Ezquerra, Michael de Luca, William Wisher, Steven E. de Souza
Judy, 2019, Tom Edge, Peter Quilter
King Richard, 2021, Zach Baylin
Kingsman: The Secret Service, 2014, Jane Goldman, Matthew Vaughan, Mark Millar, Dave Gibbons
Knives Out, 2019, Rian Johnson
Kramer vs Kramer, 1979, Avery Corman, Robert Benton, Jay Christian
Lethal Weapon, 1987, Shane Black, Jeffrey Boam
Liar Liar, 1997, Paul Guay, Stephen Mazur
Little Miss Sunshine, 2006, Michael Arndt
Logan, 2017, James Mangold, Scott Frank, Michael Green
Lord of the Rings: The Fellowship of the Ring, 2001, J.R.R. Tolkein, Fran Walsh, Phillipa Boyens, Peter Jackson
Lost in Translation, 2003, Sophia Coppola
Madagascar, 2005, Mark Burton, Billy Frolick, Eric Darnell
Magnolia, 1999, Paul Thomas Anderson
Magnum Force, 1973, Harry Julian Fink, Rita M. Fink, John Milius, Michael Cimino
Mandela, 2021, Madonne Ashwin
Memories of Murder, 2003, Bong Joon Ho, Kwang-rim Kim, Sung-bo Shim
Memento, 2000, Christopher Nolan, Jonathan Nolan

Midsommar, 2019, Ari Aster
Mission Impossible, 1996, Bruce Geller, David Koepp, Steven Zaillian, Robert Towne
Moneyball, 2011, Steven Zaillian, Aaron Sorkin, Stan Chervin
Monsters, 2010, Gareth Edwards
Murder on the Orient Express, 2017, Michael Green, Agatha Christie
Nightmare Alley, 2021, Guillermo del Toro, Kim Morgan, William Lindsay Gresham
No Time to Die, 2021, Neal Purvis, Robert Wade, Cary Joji Fukanaga, Phoebe Waller-Bridge
Nomadland, 2020, Chloé Zhao, Jessica Bruder
Nope, 2022, Jordan Peele
O Brother, Where Art Thou?, 2000, Homer, Ethan Coen, Joel Coen
Ocean's Eleven, 2001, George Clayton Johnson, Jack Golden Russell, Harry Brown
One Flew over the Cuckoo's Nest, 1975, Lawrence Hauben, Bo Goldman, Ken Kesey
Oppenheimer, 2023, Christopher Nolan, Kai Bird, Martin Sherwin
Palm Springs, 2020, Andy Siara, Max Barbakow
Panic Room, 2002, David Koepp
Passengers, 2016, Jon Spaihts
Pirates of the Caribbean: The Curse of the Black Pearl, 2003, Ted Elliott, Terry Rossio, Stuart Beattie, Jay Wolpert
Portrait of a Woman on Fire, 2019, Céline Sciamma
Primer, 2004, Shane Carruth
Promising Young Woman, 2020, Emerald Fennell
Prospect, 2018, Christopher Caldwell, Zeek Earl
Pulp Fiction, 1994, Quentin Tarantino, Roger Avary
Raiders of the Lost Ark, 1981, Lawrence Kasdan, George Lucas, Philip Kaufman
Rain Man, 1988, Barry Morrow, Ron Bass
Rear Window, 1954, John Michael Hayes, Cornell Woolrich
Riders of Justice, 2020, Anders Thomas Jensen, Nikolaj Arcel
RoboCop, 1987, Edward Neumeier, Michael Miner
Rocky, 1976, Sylvester Stallone
Rogue One: A Star Wars Story, 2016, Chris Weitz, Tony Gilroy, John Knoll, Gary Whitta, George Lucas
Room, 2015, Emma Donoghue
Saw, 2004, Leigh Whannell, James Wan
Se7en, 1995, Andrew Kevin Walker
See How They Run, 2022, Mark Chappell
Selma, 2014, Paul Webb
Serenity, 2005, Joss Whedon
Seven Samurai, 1954, Akira Kurosawa, Shinobu Hashimoto, Hideo Oguni
Shadow, 2018, Wei Li, Yimou Zhang, Sujin Zhu
Shazam!, 2019, Henry Gayden, Darren Lemke, Bill Parker
Sinbad and the Eye of the Tiger, 1977, Beverley Cross, Ray Harryhausen
Singin' in the Rain, 1952, Betty Comden, Adolph Green
Sorry to Bother You, 2018, Boots Riley
Sound of Metal, 2019, Darius Marder, Abraham Marder, Derek Cianfrance
Spider-Man: No Way Home, 2021, Chris McKenna, Erik Sommers, Stan Lee, Steve Ditko
Spirited Away, 2001, Hayao Miyazaki
Stalker, 1979, Arkadiy Strugatskiy, Boris Strugatskiy, Andrei Tarkovsky

Stan and Ollie, 2018, Jeff Pope, A.J. Marriot
Star Wars: Episode IV: A New Hope, 1977, George Lucas
Star Wars: Episode VII - The Force Awakens, 2015, Lawrence Kasdan, J.J Abrams, Michael Arnd
Star Wars: Episode VIII - The Last Jedi, 2017, Rian Johnson, George Lucas
Suffragette, 2015, Abi Morgan
Suicide Squad, 2016, David Ayer, John Ostrander
Tár, 2022, Todd Field
Terminator 2: Judgment Day, 1991, James Cameron, William Wisher
The Alamo, 1960, James Edward Grant
The Batman, 2022, Matt Reeves, Peter Craig, Bob Kane
The Beach, 2000, John Hodge, Alex Garland
The Big Trail, 1930, Hal G. Evarts, Marie Boyle, Jack Peabody
The Blair Witch Project, 1999, Daniel Myrick, Eduardo Sanchez, Heather Donahue
The Cabin in the Woods, 2011, Joss Whedon, Drew Goddard
The Dark Knight Rises, 2012, Jonathan Nolan, Christopher Nolan, David S. Goyer
The Dark Tower, 2017, Akiva Goldsman, Jeff Pinkner, Anders Thomas Jensen, Nikolaj Arcel, Stephen King
The Day the Earth Stood Still, 2008, David Scarpa, Edmund H. North
The Fast and the Furious, 2001, Ken Li, Gary Scott Thompson, Erik Bergquist, David Ayer
The Father, 2020, Christopher Hampton, Florian Zeller
The Favourite, 2018, Deborah Davis, Tony McNamara
The Godfather, 1972, Mario Puzo, Francis Ford Coppola
The Good Boss, 2021, Fernando Leon de Aranoa
The Good, the Bad and the Ugly, 1966, Luciano Vincenzoni, Sergio Leone, Agenore Incrocci, Furio Scarpelli
The Great K & A Train Robbery, 1926, Paul Leicester Ford, John Stone
The Guns of Navarone, 1961, Alistair MacLean, Carl Foreman
The Imitation Game, 2014, Graham Moore, Andrew Hodges
The Incredible Hulk, 2008, Zak Penn, Stan Lee, Jack Kirby
The Karate Kid, 1984, Robert Mark Kamen
The Lost Daughter, 2021, Maggie Gyllenhaal, Elena Ferrante
The Magnificent Seven, 1960, William Roberts, Akira Kurosawa, Walter Bernstein, Shinobu Hashimoto, Walter Newman, Hideo Oguni
The Man Who Fell to Earth, 1976, Paul Mayersberg, Walter Tevis
The Matrix, 1999, Lily Wachowski, Lana Wachowski
The Peanut Butter Falcon, 2019, Tyler Nilson, Michael Schwartz
The Power of the Dog, 2021, Jane Campion, Thomas Savage
The Princess Bride, 1987, William Goldman
The Pursuit of Happyness, 2006, Steve Conrad
The Red Shoes, 1948, Hans Christian Anderson, Emeric Pressburger, Keith Winter
The Shawshank Redemption, 1994, Stephen King, Frank Darabont
The Shining, 1980, Stephen King, Stanley Kubrick, Diane Johnson
The Silence of the Lambs, 1991, Thomas Harris, Ted Tally
The Sixth Sense, 1999, M. Night Shyamalan
The Thing, 1982, Bill Lancaster, John W. Campbell Jr.
The Truman Show, 1998, Andrew Niccol
The Whale, 2022, Samuel D. Hunter
The Wizard of Oz, 1939, Noel Langley, Florence Ryerson, Edgar Allan Woolf

The Worst Person in the World, 2021, Eskil Vogt, Joachim Trier
The Wrestler, 2008, Robert Siegel
Thelma and Louise, 1991, Callie Khouri
Thor, 2011, Ashley Millar, Zack Stentz, Don Payne
Three Billboards Outside Ebbing, Missouri, 2017, Martin McDonagh
Timecrimes, 2007, Nacho Vigalondo
Titane, 2021, Julia Ducournau, Jacques Akchoti, Simonetta Greggio
To Kill a Mockingbird, 1962, Harper Lee, Horton Foote
Tombstone, 1993, Kevin Jarre
Total Recall, 1990, Philip K. Dick, Ronald Shusett, Dan O'Bannon
Toy Story, 1995, John Lasseter, Pete Docter, Andrew Stanton
Trading Places, 1983, Timothy Harris, Herschel Weingrod
Uncharted, 2022, Rafe Judkins, Art Marcum, Matt Holloway
Under the Skin, 2013, Walter Campbell, Jonathan Glazer, Michel Faber
Unforgiven, 1992, David Webb Peoples
WALL-E, 2008, Andrew Stanton, Pete Docter, Jim Reardon
West Side Story, 1961, Ernest Lehman, Arthur Laurents, Jerome Robbins
Whiplash, 2014, Damien Chazelle
Willy Wonka and the Chocolate Factory, 1971, Roald Dahl, David Seltzer
Witness, 1985, William Kelley, Pamela Wallace, Earl W. Wallace

TV

Altered Carbon, (2018-2020), Laeta Kalogridis
Band of Brothers, (2001)
Banshee, (2013-2016), David Schickler, Jonathan Tropper
Barry, (2018-2023), Alec Berg, Bill Hader
Better Call Saul, (2015-2022), Vince Gilligan, Peter Gould
Big Love, (2006-11), Mark V. Olsen, Will Scheffer
Blake's 7, (1978-1981), Terry Nation
Bodyguard, (2018-2024), Jed Mercurio
Breaking Bad, (2008-2013), Vince Gilligan
Brooklyn Nine-Nine, (2013-2021), Dan Goor, Michael Schur
Buffy the Vampire Slayer, (1997-2003), Dan Goor, Michael Schur
Cagney and Lacey, (1981-1988), Barbara Avedon, Barbara Corday
Call the Midwife, (2012–), Heidi Thomas
Chernobyl, (2019), Craig Mazin
Cowboy Bebop, (2021), Christopher L. Yost
Curb Your Enthusiasm, (2000–), Larry David
Dad's Army, (1968-1977), Jimmy Perry
Dexter, (2006-2013), James Manos Jr.
Doctor Who, (2005–), Sydney Newman
EastEnders, (1985–), Tony Holland, Julia Smith, Tony Jordan
Fawlty Towers, (1975-1979)
Firefly, (2002-2003), Joss Whedon
Fleabag, (2016-2019), Phoebe Waller-Bridge
Friends, (1994-2004), David Crane, Marta Kauffman
Game of Thrones, (2011-2019), David Benioff, D.B. Weiss
GLOW, (2017-2019), Liz Flahive, Carly Mensch

Hap and Leonard, (2016-2018), Nick Damici, Jim Mickle
Happy Valley, (2014-2023), Sally Wainwright
Hill Street Blues, (1981-1987), Steven Bochco, Michael Kozoll
Ironside, (1967-1975), Collier Young
Jerk, (2019–), Tim Renkow, Stu Richards
Justified, 2010-2015, Graham Yost
Killing Eve, (2018-2022), Phoebe Waller-Bridge
Knight Rider, (1982-1986), Glen A. Larson
Kung Fu, (1972-1975), Ed Spielman, Herman Miller
Law and Order, (1990–)
Legion, (2017-2019), Noah Hawley
Life on Mars, (2006-2007), Matthew Graham, Tony Jordan, Ashley Pharoah
Line of Duty, (2012–), Jed Mercurio
Loki, (2021–), Michael Waldron
Lost, (2004-2010), J.J. Abrams, Jeffrey Lieber, Damon Lindelof
Mad Men, (2007-2015), Matthew Weiner
Midnight Mass, (2021), Mike Flanagan
Monkey (Saiyūki), (1978-2004), Cheng'en Wu
Monty Python's Flying Circus, (1969-1974), Graham Chapman, Eric Idle, Terry Jones
Motherland, (2016–), Sharon Horgan, Holly Walsh, Graham Linehan
Mr. Robot, (2015-2019), Sam Esmail
Nurse Jackie, (2009-2015), Liz Brixius, Evan Dunsky, Linda Wallem
Obi-Wan Kenobi, (2022–), Deborah Chow
Only Fools and Horses, (1981-2003), John Sullivan
Parks and Recreation, (2009-2015), Greg Daniels, Michael Schur
Peacemaker, (2022–), James Gunn
Peaky Blinders, (2013-2022), Steven Knight
Preacher, (2016-2019), Sam Catlin, Evan Goldberg, Seth Rogan
Quantum Leap, (1989-1993), Donald P. Bellisario
Queer as Folk, (2000-2005), Ron Cowen, Daniel Lipman, Russell T. Davies
Reacher, (2022–), Rick Santora
Rev., (2010-2014), James Wood, Tom Hollander
Russian Doll, (2019–), Leslye Headland, Natasha Lyonne, Amy Poelher
Seinfeld, (1989-1998), Larry David, Jerry Seinfeld
Severance, (2022–), Dan Erickson
Shameless, (2004-2013), Paul Abbott
Silk, (2011-2014), Peter Moffat
Sister Wives, (2010–), Puddle Monkey Productions and Figure 8 Films
Sledge Hammer!, (1986-1988), Alan Spencer
Stan Against Evil, (2016–2018), Dana Gould
Stath Lets Flats, (2018–), Jamie Demetriou, Al Roberts, Natasha Demetriou
Stranger Things, (2016-2025)
Squid Game, (2021–), Hwang Dong-hyuk
Succession, (2018-2023), Jesse Armstrong
Superman and Lois, (2021–), Greg Berlanti, Todd Helbing
Superstore, (2015-2021), Justin Spitzer
Teachers, (2001-2004), Tim Loane
Ted Lasso, (2020-2023), Brendan Hunt, Joe Kelly, Bill Lawrence
The Bay, (2019–), Daragh Carville, Richard Clark

The Big Bang Theory, (2007-2019), Chuck Lorre, Bill Prady
The Boys, (2019–), Eric Kripke
The Crown, (2016-2023), Peter Morgan
The Last of Us, (2023–), Neil Druckmann, Craig Mazin
The L Word, (2004-2009), Michele Abbott, Ilene Chaiken, Kathy Greenberg
The Life and Legend of Wyatt Earp, (1955-1961)
The Office, (2001-2003), Ricky Gervais, Stephen Merchant
The Queen's Gambit, (2020–), Scott Frank, Allan Scott
The Repair Shop, (2017–)
The Responder, (2022–), Tony Schumacher
The Sandman, (2022–), Neil Gaiman, David S. Goyer, Allan Heinberg
The Shield, (2002-2008), Shawn Ryan
The Sopranos, (1999-2007), David Chase
The Umbrella Academy, (2019-2024), Steve Blackman, Jeremy Slater
The Walking Dead, (2010-2022), Frank Darabont
The Wire, (2002-2008), David Simon
The X Files, (1993-2018), Chris Carter
True Blood, (2008-2014), Alan Ball
Westworld, (2016-2022), Lisa Joy, Jonathan Nolan
Wolf Hall, (2005)
Yellowstone, (2018–), John Linson, Taylor Sheridan

PLAYS

Bluebird, Simon Stephens, 1998
Cell Mates, Simon Gray, 1995
Firewall, Merlin Goldman, 2007
Jerusalem, Jez Butterworth, 2009
John, Annie Baker, 2015
Lemons Lemons Lemons Lemons Lemons, Sam Steiner, 2015
Macbeth, William Shakespeare, 1606
The Girl Who Was Very Good at Lying, Eoin McAndrew, 2021
Waiting for Godot, Samuel Beckett, 1952

BOOKS & COMICS

Alice's Adventures in Wonderland, Lewis Carroll, 1865
Detective Comics #27, DC Comics, 1939
Don Quixote, Miguel de Cervantes, 1605
Dracula, Bram Stoker, 1897
Dream of the Red Chamber, Cao Xueqin, Philip Bates, 2013
Eleanor Oliphant is Completely Fine, Gail Honeyman, 2017
Firestorm, the Nuclear Man, DC Comics, 1978
Foundation, Isaac Asimov, 1951
Gadsby, Ernest Vincent Wright, 1939
Inspector Rebus series, Ian Rankin, 1987
Into the Woods, John Yorke, 2014

Iron Man, DC Comics, 1968
Jin Ping Mei, Lanling Xiaoxiao Sheng, 1368
Journey to the West, Wu Cheng'en, 2014
Lord of the Flies, William Golding, 1954
Of Mice and Men, John Steinbeck, 1937
NIV Holy Bible, Biblica, 2011
Romance of the Three Kingdoms, Luo Guanzhong, He Yun, Jay Ramsay, Victoria Finlay, 2018
Save the Cat, Blake Snyder, 2005
Story, Robert McKee, 1999
The Archetypes and the Collective Unconscious, C.G Jung, 1959
The Boy Who Cried Wolf, Aesop's Fables, Aesop, 1484
The Girl Who Lied, Sue Fortin, 2023
The Hero with a Thousand Faces, Joseph Campbell, 1949
The Incredible Hulk, Marvel Comics, 1962
The Invisible Man, H. G. Wells, 1897
The Murderbot Diaries, Martha Wells, 2017
The Pilgrim's Progress, John Bunyan, 1678
The Poetics of Aristotle, Aristotle, S.H. Butcher, 2011
The Sandman, Neil Gaiman, 1989
The Vorrh, B. Catling, 2012
The Water Margin, Shi Nai'an, J.H. Jackson, Edwin Lowe, 2010
The Writer's Journey: Mythic Structure for Writers, Christopher Vogler, 2020
What to Listen for in Music, Aaron Copland, 2011
X-Men, Marvel Comics, 2010

SONGS

Dakota, Stereophonics, 2005
Half Moon Street, Pete and the Pirates, 2011
Horseshoe Crab, Slothrust, 2016
Montreal, The Wedding Present, 1997
Rise, John Lydon, 1986
Severed, The Decemberists, 2018

MISCELLANEOUS

Kurt Vonnegut on the Shapes of Stories, YouTube, May 20, 2021
　　https://www.youtube.com/watch?v=oP3c1h8v2ZQ
Paul Schrader | BAFTA Screenwriters' Lecture Series, YouTube, July 18, 2019,
　　https://www.youtube.com/watch?v=3NhSZ6RTQgk
RoboCop (1987) Is an Almost Perfectly Symmetrical Film, Deja Reviewer,
　　April 29, 2022 https://dejareviewer.com/
Storysaurus, Amy Rosenthal, Moniack Mhor, September 20, 2021

CLOUD OF FLAWS

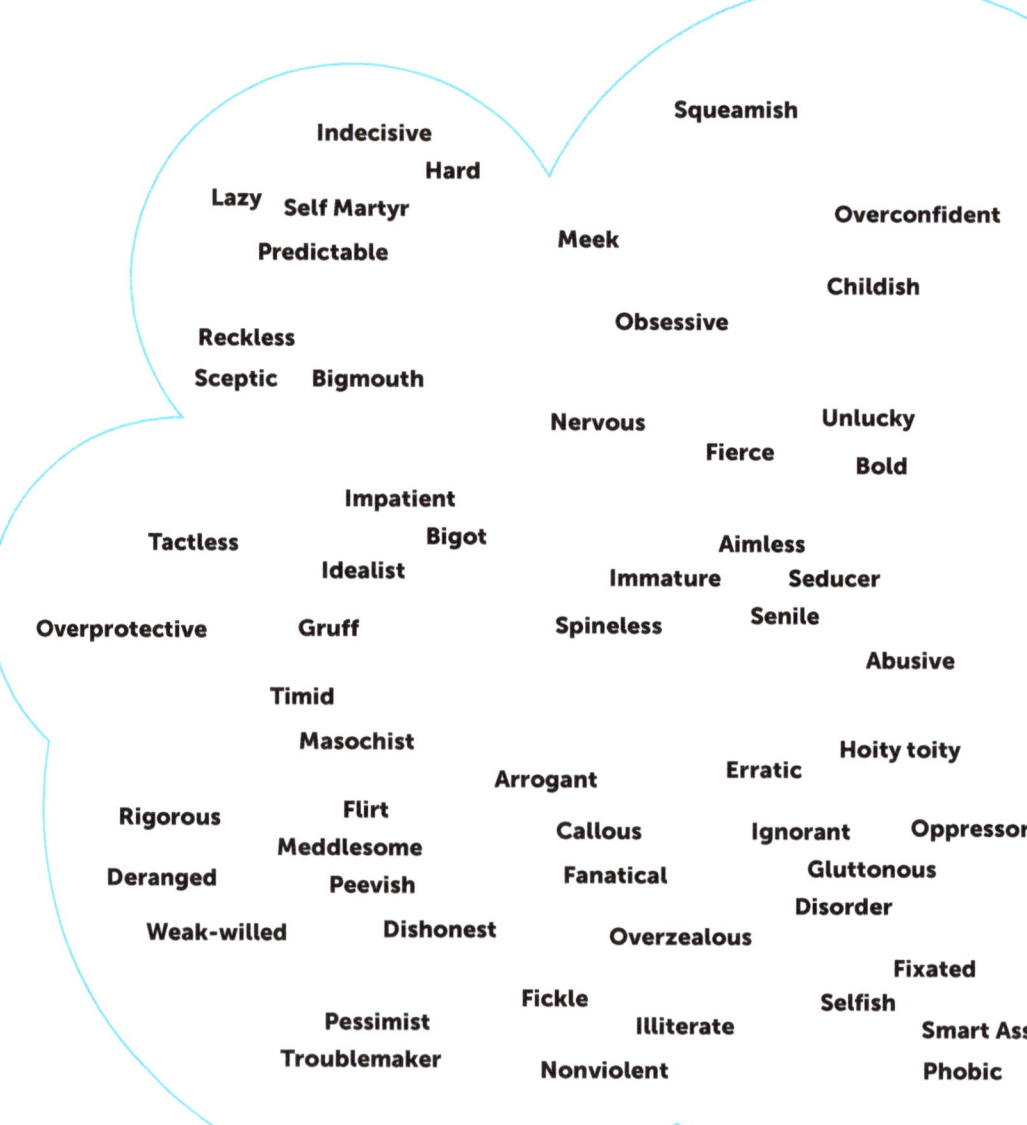

Squeamish
Indecisive
Hard
Lazy Self Martyr   Overconfident
         Meek
Predictable   Childish
              Obsessive
Reckless
Sceptic Bigmouth
           Nervous   Unlucky
                    Fierce
                             Bold
       Impatient
Tactless   Bigot   Aimless
       Idealist   Immature   Seducer
Overprotective Gruff Spineless Senile
                                  Abusive
       Timid
       Masochist
              Arrogant   Erratic   Hoity toity
Rigorous Flirt
       Meddlesome   Callous   Ignorant Oppressor
Deranged Peevish   Fanatical   Gluttonous
                                Disorder
Weak-willed   Dishonest   Overzealous
                                   Fixated
              Fickle   Selfish
       Pessimist   Illiterate
       Troublemaker Nonviolent   Smart Ass
                                   Phobic

Vain Liar Paranoid Pest
Untrustworthy Hypocritical
Finicky Megalomaniac
Soft-hearted Cruel
Unpredictable Self-righteous Incompetent
Dubious Cursed Disloyal
Envious Idiotic Rebellious
Anxious Humourless
Judgmental Alcoholic
Sarcastic Dyslexic Spiteful
Solemn Naïve Dependent Audacious Superstitious
Absentminded Nosey Tongue-tied
Complex Pacifist
Addict Overemotional Blunt
Zealous
Overambitious
Impious Bad Habits Practical Withdrawn
Hedonistic Egotistical Shallow Stubborn
Sadist Impish
Intolerant Lustful Remorseless
Gullible Disturbed Perfectionist
Proud Infamy Indifferent Lewd Theatrical

Appendix. 257

CHARACTER ARCHETYPES

	EGO			FREEDOM		
	MAGICIAN	HERO	CREATOR	EXPLORER	REBEL	JESTER
Goal	Fulfil dreams	Improve world	Realise vision	Fulfilment	Overturn	Have a great time
Skill	Win-win	Courage	Creativity	Autonomy	Radical	Joy
Flaw	Manipulative	Arrogance	Perfection	Misfit	Crime	Frivolity
Fear	Neg outcomes	Vulnerability	Mediocrity	Conformity	Powerless	Being bored

Table 14: Character Archetypes.

	SOCIAL			ORDER			
	LOVER	**CAREGIVER**	**EVERYMAN**	**INNOCENT**	**RULER**	**SAGE**	
	Relationship	Help others	To belong	Be happy	Success	Find truth	Goal
	Passion	Compassion	Realism	Optimism	Leadership	Wisdom	Skill
	Lose identity	Exploited	Losing self	Boring	Authoritarian	Never act	Flaw
	Being alone	Selfishness	Left out	Doing wrong	Chaos	Being misled	Fear

ACKNOWLEDGEMENTS

The author would like to thank all those who have helped to support the writing and publication of this book. In particular, the author would like to thank beta readers Jo Ullah, Fiona Hunnisett, Rebecca Franks, and Desi Lyon. The support of the Bristol Writing Group (Knight Writers) and Sonya Newland is also much appreciated. The book also wouldn't be possible without some of the many tutors, colleagues, and mentors I've had over the years, including Lyndon Ives, Rachel Aspinall, Michael Lengsfield, Emma Earle, Fiona Hamilton, Phillip Shelley, Howard Brenton, James Fritz, Louis Savy, Darren Rapier, Evan Placey, Elinor Cook, Russell Gascoigne, Ryan Craig, Jacob Ross, Karol Griffiths, Alison Hennessey, Simon Stephens, Mike Bullen, Matt Grinter, John Warren, Alexie Basil, Adam Schaller, Chris Jones, Bob Schulz, Lucy Hay, Katherine Stansfield, John Yorke, Robin Mukherjee, Linda Aronson, Gillian Greer, Vicki Jung, Lisa Parry, and LSF's Talent Campus 5.

www.ingramcontent.com/pod-product-compliance
Lightning Source LLC
Chambersburg PA
CBHW041305110526
44590CB00028B/4248